A Single Mum's Journey

A Single Mum's Journey

Personal testimony and practical advice to encourage and support

Jo Drower

A Single Mum's Journey
Published by Jo Drower
New Zealand

ISBN 978-0-473-47102-6 (Softcover)
ISBN 978-0-473-47103-3 (ePUB)
ISBN 978-0-473-47104-0 (Kindle)

Editing: Sue Beguely

Production & Typesetting:
Andrew Killick
Castle Publishing Services
www.castlepublishing.co.nz

Cover design:
Paul Smith

To Jessie and Jack
Thank you for our amazing journey.
You are a great gift from God.

Contents

Introduction

Recently I celebrated ten years' walking with Jesus. As I reflected on the day I gave my life to follow Him, I recalled I knew so little but understood I needed to take this first step. Now I am overwhelmed with gratitude and I hope you will find the following pages a testimony to that. Had I not decided to follow Jesus I do not know where I, or my children, would be today. Left to myself I was vulnerable to alcohol, drugs and guys who liked the same. But fortunately I was converted and it was the greatest thing that has ever happened to me. Therefore, I would like to spend the rest of my life sharing this good news and encouraging others. I sincerely hope you will enjoy reading about this journey of a single mum and that you will be encouraged to reflect on your own journey.

I am still surprised I so much wanted to write a book on the years I fumbled my way through single parenting. I must confess I haven't always had the focus on my children that I encourage in these chapters. I spent the first three years of my journey completely self-focused and captured by regular bouts of binge drinking. I was vulnerable to the destructive lifestyle I had known in my youth. It was through God's grace and patience that my life was transformed. God is all about transformation. He is continually changing me to be patient instead of self-focused, kind instead of harsh, forgiving rather than authoritarian. God teaches how to parent children in harmony rather than by ranting. He gives the freedom and desire to learn effective parenting and the knowledge to raise children who will ultimately live in obedience to Him. It is my prayer that you will see the power of God's transformation in my life throughout the pages of this book. Because if He can do that for me, He can do that for anyone.

I hope this book will encourage and strengthen you in your journey as a single mum. I will always be grateful to a dear friend who gave me a book by a single mum – the author Angela Thomas – who spoke right into my life. Angela shared about God's love for her and her single-parent family. It encouraged me to parent to the best of my ability and assured me that my family was unique. Sure, I really loved my children, but at that point in time I didn't truly value my family. A single-parent family is not ideal, and I didn't think I could faithfully raise children who would become strong in the Lord, strong in society and able to prove the negative statistics[1] wrong.

I can still recall how it felt when I made the first visit to Work and Income to apply for government assistance. I felt like a second-rate citizen, and there would continue to be times when I felt that way. Reading the journey of another single mother encouraged me. Now my children are much older, I hope to encourage you that you too can make it through the struggles, sacrifices, tears and laughter. Sure it's a hard role, but it is a role we must be faithful to even when we feel we have damaged our children beyond repair or we simply don't want to get out of bed and face another day of thankless work.

Having read Angela Thomas' book I wanted to give a Kiwi perspective on the role of single parenting as we have a culture that differs from her American way of life. Our culture has a different view of God and church. Our culture promotes rugby and beer, binge drinking and weed! I didn't grow up hearing Christians stepping up to say God wants more for us, that His standards are higher than we are setting. New Zealanders have the *tall poppy syndrome;* we can demoralise anyone stepping out from the norm to encourage others to be different. Our culture has an opinion of single mothers that is not at all honouring to women. It does not encourage us to value ourselves or our role, yet our children need the best we've got.

Regardless of how you became a single parent, I pray this book will encourage you to look at your journey with fresh hope. As I look back over the last thirteen years I thank God for the journey because I learnt so much about Him and about myself. I discovered what I truly value in life and grew passionate about being the best mum I could be. There are days when I feel I fail miserably and other days I consider quite victorious. There have been tears from strain and tears from laughter. Since becoming a member of God's family there has been a sense of excitement about His plan and purpose for myself and my children. And while we have no idea what tomorrow will bring, what is exciting is that we have the opportunity to grow where God has planted us, to be the best we can be.

I had this verse on my fridge when I started life as a single mum. I don't actually know how it came to be there! I do remember I would read it and get a sense of hope and awareness that there is a choice to how we live our lives.

> Be gracious to me, O God, be gracious to me,
> For my soul takes refuge in You;
> And in the shadow of Your wings I will take refuge

> Until destruction passes by,
> I will cry to God Most High,
> To God who accomplishes all things for me.
> He will send from heaven and save me;
> He reproaches him who tramples upon me.
> God will send forth His lovingkindness and His truth.
> (Psalm 57:1-3)

This book is a testimony to my love and gratitude for my Lord and Saviour Jesus Christ. I hope you will be inspired to be the best you can be and know that a lot of your fumbles and failings are common to all mothers. You may be bound up in lies, doubts and struggles. My own journey and role as a social worker has shown me a number of traps mums can fall into. I want you to know that you have a choice, and this choice will affect both the safety and well-being of you and your children.

It has taken a number of years to write and rewrite this book. It has been therapeutic and given me fresh insights. I would like to acknowledge the support of Jocelyn and Pete, for their hours of shaping the raw material. To Castle Publishing and John's encouraging words that what I seek to share is clear, biblical and powerful. I am so grateful. There has been a lot of editing as I would have to be the least qualified to write a book! But God never took the desire away and I believe He has guided and led me throughout. It really started to take shape when I decided to run Psalm 139 alongside the first four chapters. This psalm speaks of His awesome power and how intimately acquainted He is with each of us. I hope it speaks to you and captivates you,

> so that Christ may dwell in your hearts through faith;
> and that you, being rooted and grounded in love, may

> be able to comprehend with all the saints what is the breadth and length and height and depth, and to know the love of Christ which surpasses knowledge, that you may be filled up to all the fullness of God. (Ephesians 3:17-19)

Enjoy.
Jo Drower

Chapter 1

My Story

'Come on, Mum. Come and bounce with us ... please ...' my daughter said as she leapt around the trampoline, her hair rising and falling with each jump and catching the sunlight on that clear winter morning.

Tears came into my eyes. I wanted to, but I couldn't.

I had always been an active person and bouncing with my children on the trampoline had been something we enjoyed doing together, but suddenly the effort seemed insurmountable. There was nothing physically wrong with me; I just couldn't get my mind to work properly. My mother stood beside me supporting me, not with words, but with her presence.

It was the middle of 2002. I'd had a rough ride and I had many tough months ahead of me. Dad had died suddenly from a heart attack two months prior and Mum was to leave us in three months due to cancer of the stomach. I could still breathe ... but not much more. It took immense effort and concentration to perform my normal daily routines.

I loved my parents so much and losing them hurt unbearably. They had raised my siblings and me in a no-frills style – an easy life with lots of security, love and basic needs met. I had an easy childhood with lots of happy memories. As a teenager I was a natural academic and achieved passes in my subjects with minimal study – even horticulture which held no interest for me whatsoever. Unfortunately, when it came time to leave college and make big decisions, my parents didn't encourage me in the way I should go. I was a typical self-centred, ego-driven teenager who chose to live from one weekend to the next, concerned only with the social aspects of life. I married at 22 years of age and, although I was immature, I loved my husband. I didn't go into marriage with any idea it would fail – we don't tend to put 'get divorced' on our goals list! So, typically, I didn't imagine it would happen to me.

I kept a journal and, looking at my entries prior to 2002, I see a young woman fighting to remain married, working at changing and thinking I had a successful way of viewing life.

29 September 2001

Finally I have made the decision to put pen to paper and allow my thoughts to flow out rather than just whirl around in my head.

A veil is lifting and I truly believe I am starting my life afresh. I feel I am more in control, relaxed, confident, fulfilled and in touch with me – Joanne!

I understand that I need to keep my life simple and uncluttered. I am such a fortunate person: fantastic husband and children. I come from a wonderful family and I have had so many intelligent, giving people come into my life. I now understand 'I am blessed'. I know this because I know how to learn from all the special people that surround me, which in turn helps me focus on what is most important to me – my family.

I think I've known for quite a while now how to be ful-

> filled and lead a life that is in harmony with nature. So I look back and see the signs and know I have the strength to put it together completely rather than in fits and starts.
>
> *30 September 2001*
>
> I am cured! I am no longer a dependent [on marijuana].
> Value each day with the people close to you – they may not be here tomorrow.

I was so very self-absorbed, and one aspect of that was my smoking marijuana. I justified and defended using this addictive substance as a 'naturally-grown product that helped me relax'. Over time I believe marijuana robbed me of a lot of things but family in particular. There were too many nights when my little girl just wanted to enjoy a story at bedtime but I would hurry through this 'task' so I could get out to the lounge, smoke a pipe and mellow out to a movie. My daughter had a very short-tempered mother, highly impatient and I would blame and scold her for mucking around. I wonder how she must have felt as she fell asleep some nights.

> *8 October 2001*
>
> Jessie's first day of morning kindy [kindergarten]. I was an organised mum for her ... I realised as I was driving to kindy this morning that I am no longer scared. Sounds funny, but it really feels wonderful. I don't feel so cluttered and yeah *I am no longer scared*. Thank you for letting me see this and move into a new chapter of self-discovery – it feels great!

> *10 October 2001*
>
> Well boy-oh-boy, just as quickly as a bad day sneaks up on me, so does it disappear. Yesterday I felt really down and today – great. Could it be I did the right thing by cancelling plans and staying put?
>
> *10 November 2001*
>
> Life is a funny wee thing. Some days are great and other days are just plain hard. I can't be hard on myself or my kids or, of course, my husband. We are all trying our best and most days we succeed but sometimes we don't and I must help my family by stopping it [depression], picking myself up and not allowing it to go on. I am the one who can control that – it is up to me.

Even though my dad had aged dramatically around his sixtieth birthday and had developed crippling arthritic-like symptoms, actually hearing the words at the other end of the phone saying, 'Dad died at six o'clock this morning' just didn't seem real. It was 9 March and what happened over the following weeks was a nightmare, which I'll talk more about later.

> *31 March 2002*
>
> Well I've been to hell and back! Reading these pages I see the signs were there back then. I am on 24-hour release from Te Awhina (a rest-home for the mentally unwell). Who would have guessed it! The support has been overwhelming. My freezer is loaded with meals and offers of

> assistance are, [as the saying goes ...] coming out of my husband's ears. Again the message rings home: *keep life simple* – enjoy the basics, especially family. Family isn't around forever. I finish this chapter of my life, tears welling, with the simple words 'I love you Dad more than I ever realised – I miss you, beautiful man.'

The last time I smoked marijuana was the night I came home from being in a psychiatric unit, which was a couple of weeks after Dad died. As you can imagine, weed did not go well with the medication I was given by the hospital or with my state of mind at that time. I had been hooked for sixteen years but that was to be my last puff.

Then Mum was gone too ...

> *31 August 2002*
>
> Sometimes life can be brutally hard.
>
> It is two weeks since Mum died and I miss her so very, very much. Initially I was grateful she was no longer suffering with the cancer, but now, in its place, is pure loneliness for a woman I truly adored.

When it came to dealing with Mum's death I turned to food for comfort and poured on a lot of weight.

> *12 December 2002*
>
> I am so overwhelmed with grief. With Mum and Dad gone there is a huge void, an emptiness that no one except my brothers and sister can truly understand.

> I am overwhelmed by the suddenness of it all, the finality it brings and because time with the two most special people in my life is now over.
>
> For too long now I have felt that the enormity of it is suffocating me and I am really struggling. And I mean *really* struggling. I can hide it from people but I don't know if that is healthy. Yet it is difficult for my husband and friends to understand as they still have their parents and they may resent being reminded that one day they will face this too.
>
> Luckily I have support, people I can ring, so I don't feel alone. I just feel so very sad. I loved my parents so much. I miss them.

Then, towards the end of December, my marriage ended as well.

I'd been through enough – 2002 had been a horrible year – full of many of life's major stressors. My sister and I reflected upon this and called it *living life in the grey*. After our parents died, life no longer seemed black and white.

Change is difficult: swapping the comfortable for the uncomfortable with its uncertainties and doubts. Often we may intend to change but change doesn't eventuate. Then there are times when we have no choice. After 2002 I learnt what it is like to be picked up and drop kicked out of my comfort zone, never to return!

When I became a single mum I lost interest in food and moved on to alcohol. There were a few years of binge drinking when the children were at their dad's for the weekend.

Sometimes there has been such a keen awareness that I was 'doing life on my own.' For example, the visit to Work and

Income for living assistance; having to cope alone with a child having a febrile convulsion; and planning family holidays. I went through a stage when I would get really annoyed every time I saw a 'perfect' woman sitting in the passenger seat as her 'perfect' husband drove their 'perfect' car. I think what helped get me through the first year was having routine in the home; this also allowed me to become a university student. I had asked Mum two years prior to her death why I was never encouraged into tertiary studies. She responded in terms of how she and Dad felt about university but, for me, I felt I had missed out on something I needed to do. On the last weekend I had with her, I told her I wanted to study to be a counsellor, so I could listen to other people's hard times, a welcome relief from my own!

So in 2003 I took my first paper as a test and I loved it. The children would be in bed by 7.30pm and then I would lay all the supplementary reading books over the lounge floor. I felt if I had not occupied myself with something, the television would have become my companion on those lonely nights flying solo when the children were little and needed early nights. I now have a social work degree and look back on seven years of study which, although it was hard at times, has been so very worthwhile.

When a marriage initially splits, emotions can be raw for a number of months. Yet, in my case, I had left the marriage so I also felt a sense of freedom. The year prior had been so difficult that not having a husband around to blame or despise meant I just got on with things. I got busy with study, sewing and looking after my children. Then I decided to buy a house.

Becoming a single person again meant finding a new identity. I enjoyed the distraction of 'finding myself' but I was to learn that grief waits – it doesn't go away while we are busy avoiding it. So when I ended up sitting in a church pew a couple of years later, I could not hide my grief – God sees all. Even today when I am struggling or sad and I come before the Lord in prayer, the tears and emotions just flow out because with Him there is no hiding. God is real and we just simply cannot fake it. He knows exactly what we are thinking and exactly what our motives are (1 Chronicles 28:9). He drew me to Himself and revealed Himself to me through His Word, the Bible and, in time I would reach out and receive His amazing grace and love. The journal entries for 2001 highlight what a prideful person I was. On the one hand I would tick the census box for Christianity based on my belief in God yet, on the other hand, I did not feel worthy to sit in a church pew. When I started to attend church it was to take my children to Sunday school and I stayed out back with them. There was no way a terrible heathen person such as myself was going to sit amongst the good Christian folk. To this day I don't actually know how it came about that a couple of months later I was sitting in a pew. These journal entries show how I fought against making a commitment to God:

> *25 September 2005*
>
> Today I went to church heavily hung over! My morning had consisted of being sick, very sick. I very nearly did not go to church as I had to speak on behalf of our group about '40 days of purpose' [a weekly study that was being held at my home]. Twice I nearly rung my leaders as I felt sooo ill. I could imagine my mum telling me not to be so hard on myself. I rang my sister to discuss part of what I wanted to say at church and I could hear stern disappointment in her voice – though nothing that compared to how I had been berating myself.

At church the worship leader mentioned the psalm, 'The Lord is my Shepherd' which had been on my fridge since 2003 before I started attending church. What an amazing journey I began when I started to attend church. What a wonderful church, filled with beautiful people. Thank you Lord for bringing my neighbour into my life – the day I went to church with her was the best thing that could have happened to me. I have learnt so much about myself from this episode; I have to use it as a big learning curve.

Lord I am not ready to approach the *born again* issue, and I know a day will come when you insist that I do. You are so loving and patient. I am not worthy of all you do for me but I think and feel that you believe I am worth it because I want so very much to please you, but this journey is too important to rush – right! I like to think I am savouring each moment and You are giving me some amazing moments. I thank you God with all I am.

19 December 2005

As I prepare to write down goals for 2006 I feel this year has prepared me in many ways. I did not find the romance relationship I had listed in my 2005 goals, instead I found a much better relationship, one that gives me more love than I would ever have imagined. I no longer walk alone. Although I don't believe I ever did, I feel guided and more fulfilled to 'captain my ship' and lead a healthier, happier life. My weakness has been drinking so with that in mind, my goals are ...

13 May 2006

What a year this is! My brother shared with me what it means to be saved. I had no idea. Although I read the Bible daily and learn lots, I am so aware that I know very little! I am so very grateful that I am on a path that is pleasing to God.

Drinking is no longer an issue. Life is simpler for me now and I am full of gratitude. All I want is to work for God, helping others via my profession as a social worker and leading them to God's salvation.

A poem that I thought of this morning:

Once there was fear, but now there is hope,
Once there was selfishness but now gratefulness.
Once despair but now a longing to serve.
I felt so alone but now I have strength and courage.
All the glory is to God

The day I gave my life to Jesus I lost all desire to drink. This is the journal entry of my draft testimony which I wrote in preparation for my baptism on Sunday, 2 July:

I am pleased to give my testimony today as it is a tribute to God's love and patience. He brings us through hardships to be a stronger person if we just let go and give it all to Him. I know He will never fail me. In my childhood we went to church occasionally. I remember praying a lot and learning about God when I was seven when a 'moving church' came to school. But there was no follow-through. Being married in a church and

> christening my children were important in terms of my beliefs at the time. In fact I drifted through life not really giving religion much thought and certainly not pleasing God. But four years ago my dad died suddenly and so much changed for me. I broke down. This event showed me that without God I could not cope, but with God I can. With God I can cope and I feel a strong call to help others cope.

Surprisingly my final version didn't have any of the above but I thought it worth mentioning.

As I look back on these journal entries, I am surprised to see I considered my breakdown had the greatest impact of all that happened that year. Surprised because out of the four big events that occurred I now feel that was the least of them. In fact if I had to put them in order I would say the biggest was my mum's death and the loss of my marriage. My mum's death because I still miss her so much. I absolutely miss Dad too, but there was a closeness with my mum that has left a huge void in my life. Upon reflection, grief is such an ongoing journey whereas my psychotic episode was just that, an episode. It was an amazingly freakish thing and I learnt a lot about the brain and the importance of sleep. Oddly enough I am now thankful for the experience as I can connect easily with those who have had similar experiences.

Secondly, my marriage would come next, because I am often reminded of the difficulty it has caused my children. Every now and then the children will verbalise the fallout and I am very thankful they can do this. Children need to be able to share and we need to listen to what they say otherwise they do not get an opportunity to hear words such as 'I am sorry. Please forgive me;

I acted very selfishly at the time' and 'There was nothing you did that caused your parents to separate.' Children can blame themselves; they can form a negative mindset and some might resort to unhealthy behaviours such as drinking, cutting and drugs as their 'medication' to numb the pain. Some may remain angry and struggle to form healthy relationships. It is painful to see the hurt that divorce brings to children, especially in the early teens when they seek to find their own identity in life. But we cannot change the past. For children whose parent has died or who have only ever known one parent, there are many struggles and questions for them to share and seek answers to. We must give our children hope and truth for the future. The ultimate hope is in Christ Jesus and the truth is in God's Word.

> I thank Christ Jesus our Lord, who has strengthened me, because He considered me faithful, putting me into service, even though I was formerly a blasphemer and a persecutor and a violent aggressor. Yet I was shown mercy because I acted ignorantly in unbelief; and the grace of our Lord was more than abundant, with the faith and love which are found in Christ Jesus. It is a trustworthy statement, deserving full acceptance, that Christ Jesus came into the world to save sinners, among whom I am foremost of all. Yet for this reason I found mercy, so that in me as the foremost, Jesus Christ might demonstrate His perfect patience as an example for those who would believe in Him for eternal life. Now to the King eternal, immortal, invisible, the only God, be honor and glory forever and ever. Amen. (1 Timothy 1:12-17)

27 August 2009

Wow! I look back over these pages of the journal and thank God for bringing me to this day. In particular I note that I wrote in December 2005 that I 'captain my ship'. But, in fact, Jesus captains my ship and I just want to sit and watch with joy and gratefulness this beautiful Lord in action.

I love times like this morning when I can sit at His feet [reading the Bible] as lately I have been really busy – not that I am complaining, it is a joy to serve. But with the busyness it is also necessary to find time to be still before Him.

I do not feel inclined to write goals, ask or wish for anything as that takes away from the contentment in all that God has given. There is soooo much.

Thank you Lord for the gift of motherhood, the gift of serving You, the gift of love, the gift of family, the gift of life and the liberty that comes with it. All I am and all I have is because of You.

I have always shared with my children, since they were young, that there is every possibility they can have great marriages – every possibility they can give their own children the opportunity to be raised in a loving two-parent home. I have sought opportunities to talk about their future and encourage them to be the type of adult they aspire to.

As a parent who has known addiction and who has worked with families dealing with addictions, I see how much our children are robbed of knowing us. We are robbed of knowing ourselves. Addiction tells our children that something is more important than they are. Addiction is also selfishness. In our society we have no problem naming the seriousness of drug and alcohol addiction, gambling and pornography, and rightly so. But there are other addictions that I'm going to call 'respectable addictions' which are also detrimental. The most obvious one is work, employment-type work that gives a parent status, wealth and, in some cases, a means of avoiding the hard task of parenting.

As a single parent you are the only adult in the home so I want to encourage you to examine yourself. Are there any addictions robbing you of time away from your children? Is it a respectable addiction that you need to name out loud and deal with – such as social media, computer games, an ultra-clean home or exercise? Is there anything that may be telling your children 'this is more important than you'?

Chapter 2

He Knows Me

I was the single mother who had mess shoved under the beds and all over the floor. My children's drawers were overloaded with clothes they had outgrown two seasons ago! I really enjoyed being the mum of my two young children but there were things I really struggled with. One in particular was family holidays. When my parents died and I reflected on childhood memories, the ones that stood out the most were holidays, often at camping grounds. I have met one amazing single mum of seven who took her children around Europe! I recall just the one holiday in my first five years as a single mum.

It was February 2004 and I took my daughter to the Gold Coast in Australia. We stayed with friends and had a blast at Dreamworld and Movie World. This actually turned out to be a very important trip for me. It was over a year since the death of my parents and the separation. So much had continued to happen including starting university and purchasing my first house. I did hide a lot of grief, buried it down so I didn't have to face it – I had no idea how. My daughter and I got on a rollercoaster ride at Movie World where our legs were dangling and our torsos were harnessed into the seat. For the initial part of the ride I was screaming from a mixture of fear and excitement. I imagined my mum saying 'shut your mouth' (a wee joke we shared as she had false teeth and was once told to shut her mouth or they might fall out). When I closed my mouth and stopped screaming I began to really enjoy the sensation of the ride, so much so that I was just buzzing after that. When we returned home I searched for amusement parks around the world with a strong desire to get a regular fix of rollercoaster sensation! Yeah, that never happened.

Quite a bit of tension left me from that trip to Australia. I reflected that just a year or so prior, I had struggled to bounce on our trampoline. Also the university studies I started half way through 2003 gave me a different focus. I began with a certificate in counselling theory and found the material was helping me to put some thoughts into perspective and take a more mature view of my situation. Unfortunately, although I mostly coped through the week, the weekends when my children weren't home I would drink up a storm. I am thankful I was kept safe through this dark period of plunging myself into drunken, senseless states.

As I shared in the first chapter, I entered a church in 2004 because I wanted my children to attend Sunday school. On one hand I was full of pride in who I was and what I was achieving yet, on the other hand, I felt quite useless as a parent and hopeless as a person. I felt damaged and sad from my losses in 2002. I felt heavily burdened from making some big decisions such as buying a house, as well as by all the single day-to-day decisions for my family. I felt unworthy as a woman who had left her husband and taken their children. I had no idea what lay ahead. Past journal entries indicate I contemplated issues at a slightly deeper level: who was I and where was I at? But I don't recall ever really questioning the meaning of life and life after death.

I believed there was a higher power called God and He created the earth. I had heard Bible stories about Adam and Eve, Noah and Jonah. And for this reason I wanted to take my children to Sunday school. They had been christened as infants. And so in March 2004 I entered a small-town church to take my children to Sunday school. On the large front window of the church were the words: Where you will find the meaning of life. Well that is exactly what I found, but it would take two years before I decided to follow Jesus.

I recall one night in the midst of this two-year period; I was doing the dishes. My eight-year-old was whining constantly at my side. Fortunately, she was a good metre plus out of arm's reach. I was washing a pot and my blood started to boil in anger at her monotonous droning. I slammed the pot into the sink and turned towards her ready to unleash my fury. As I looked at my daughter, who was totally unaware of the internal battle going on in me, I had to turn away. Instead of striking her I turned and ran out of the kitchen, down the hall and, much like a teenager, I slammed the spare room door. I was in a quiet room. While I was yet to make a confession of faith and become a Christian, I made at this moment a plea with praying hands, confessing that being a single parent was too hard, that I was struggling to parent my strong-willed children. I walked out of that room with new hope! The answer to my plea, while not audible, was planted into my mind and it was simply, 'who is the adult in this home?' I made a more determined effort to take charge. I began making decisions as the adult in the home. As I say, I hadn't become a Christian at this point, but that did happen before my daughter turned nine.

When I became a Christian, studying God's Word was for me like feasting on the finest of food. I have always liked books and seen their value but there were long spells when I didn't read. As a Christian I simply could not get enough reading time and I felt I needed about three lifetimes to read all the books I wanted to! So it is a great privilege to write my own book even though it has not been an easy task. When I first read Angela Thomas' single mum story she made writing look easy. Had I not had such a strong conviction to write this book I could easily have given up. There have been times of too much of me and not enough of God; too many quotes; no flow; and the list goes on. When I prayerfully decided to underline the first four chapters with the beautiful writings of Psalm 139, I discovered not only great insights from studying Scripture but also this psalm showed me that God knew me from the beginning – little ole me! In fact it goes on to say that 'He knitted me together in my mother's womb.'

There is a lot to try and comprehend about God and our relationship to Him, so I want to share with you how I saw, through the psalm, that God knew me even in those years prior to being a Christian. Over the next two chapters I am going to share my journey from 2002 – 2006 when my life changed. Chapters 4 and 5 will address the additional changes that took place in May 2006.

Let me begin with some context to the psalm. While it is mostly agreed that David is the author of this psalm,[1] it is difficult to pinpoint at what stage of his life he wrote it. The shepherd boy David, who killed Goliath and became King of Israel, was likely born between 1040 and 1030BC.[2] David is regarded as the author of almost half of the psalms in the Bible; they are an amazing collection of songs of praise and worship to God. Psalm 139 is a song about God's omnipresence and omniscience, His being everywhere and knowing everything.

This chapter contains the first six verses which I have summarised as 'He knows me'. He knew me from the beginning. He always knew me even though I did not know Him for the first 35 years of my life.

> O LORD, You have searched me and known me.
> You know when I sit down and when I rise up;
> You understand my thought from afar.
> You scrutinize my path and my lying down,
> And are intimately acquainted with all my ways.
> Even before there is a word on my tongue,
> Behold, O LORD, You know it all.
> You have enclosed me behind and before,
> And laid Your hand upon me.
> Such knowledge is too wonderful for me;
> It is too high, I cannot attain to it. (Psalm 139:1-6)

When I first began my journey as a single mum in January 2003, I was blind, lost and separated from God. In fact the Bible has much to say about the state I was in then. The appendices at the back of my Bible lists these characteristics as:

> Hateful to God; full of evil; fully set to do evil; deceitful and wicked; far from God; prone to depart from God; impenitent; unbelieving; blind; of little worth; deceitful; hard; haughty; influenced by the devil; worldly; covetous; vengeful; ensnaring; foolish; angry toward the Lord; idolatrous; mad; mischievous; proud; rebellious; perverse; stone-hearted; arrogant; stubborn; elated by sensual indulgence; devises violence; often judicially insensitive.[3]

Wow, what a list! Yet Psalm 139:1-6 still says that He knew me, He searched me and has known me. As I read through each of the characteristics listed above I can honestly say every one of them was true of me. Even today there are some I have to work on to overcome. For example, pride still needs lots of work. I recall the first time I heard John 15:5, 'For apart from Me you can do nothing.' I was somewhat put out; I thought it a bit offensive to the good in me! I also recall that prior to my salvation my Christian brother tried to explain Christianity to me. He sounded like a mechanic explaining a motor where he had studied the manual and I hadn't. I said to him that one day I would read the Bible. I certainly was intrigued but I considered it a task to put on my 'bucket list'.

Now as I read Psalm 139, I marvel that God knew that one day I would be His. He waited patiently for the right time to show me my need for Him. In verse one it says that the Lord has searched me and known me. A great preacher in the nineteenth century, C.H. Spurgeon interprets this as follows:

> God understands us, and is most intimately acquainted with our person, nature, and character. How well it is for us to know the God who knows us! ... There was never a time in which we were unknown to God, and there never will be a moment in which we shall be beyond His observation ... How wonderful the contrast between the observer and the observed! Jehovah [God] and me! Yet this most intimate connection exists and therein lies our hope. Let the reader sit still awhile and try to realise the two poles of this statement – the Lord and poor puny man – and he will see much to admire and wonder at.[4]

I love how Spurgeon calls us 'poor puny man'. In today's 'feel-good' society we have removed these sorts of reminders and rarely hear words like that describing the true nature of man. In today's society the list of characteristics I quoted above would be abhorrent to a lot of people, yet the truth is we are all born sinners. We are all born separated from God because sin entered the world back in the Garden of Eden when Adam and Eve disobeyed God's only command. Mankind cannot do anything to earn a place with God. By faith alone we are saved, nothing of our own doing (Ephesians 2:8). (If you believe you can earn your salvation or that there is any way you can become a Christian without acknowledging your sin and turning to the full grace that is found in the death and resurrection of Jesus Christ, then I encourage you to read Appendix A at the back of this book.)

When we become a Christian, some of the natural characteristics we had as an unsaved person require time to overcome. Spurgeon writes:

> Our paths may be habitual or accidental, open or secret, but with them all the Most Holy One is well acquainted. This should fill us with awe, so that we sin not; with courage, so that we fear not; with delight, so that we mourn not.[5]

Christians, I hope you are filled with awe, courage and delight as you recall your own time of salvation. God's instructions are not burdensome (1 John 5:3). Being a Christian does not mean adhering to a list of demands and rules. At the core of Christianity are two commands: Love God and love others. But He first loved us (1 John 4:19) and He desires our love and obedience in response. I am limited in my understanding of many things, all the more of what my children experienced without their dad in the home. I never had to contemplate that growing up. It makes sense to me, when I compare my parenting prior to being a Christian to after, is that my children need God to be guiding me in my role and I need to be looking to Him to make sense of this world, for the three of us. Prior to becoming a Christian, I was totally blind. Spiritually blind that is, not physically. I was having a good time caring for my children, working and socialising – that was probably the extent of my existence.

The following diagram illustrates how we view ourselves. Either we view ourselves through the lens of the world (again not in the physical sense but the invisible spiritual sense) or through God's Word:

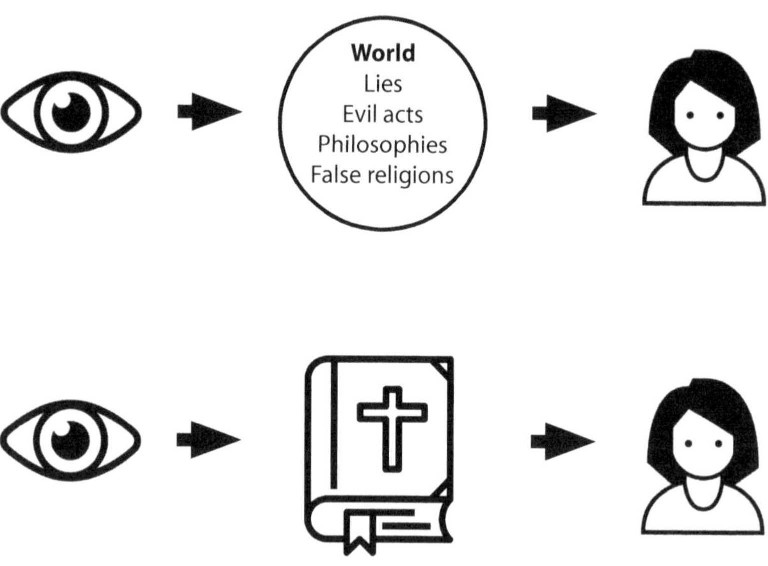

There is so much to learn about ourselves when we align who we are with the One who created us. There is so much freedom in understanding why God made us and what He wants us to be. He knows me and He knows you too. And I will be forever grateful that for two years God stripped away all desire I had to live without Him.

Psalm 139:3 says, 'You scrutinize my path and my lying down, and are intimately acquainted with all my ways'. Spurgeon writes:

> God takes notice of every step we take, every right step, and every by-step. He knows what rule we walk by, what end we walk toward, what company we walk with.[6]

While I had some wonderful friendships in the drinking days prior to salvation, I needed to distance myself from them when I was a new believer. Ultimately the days of getting drunk ended up making me aware of how lost and useless I was, how little control I had over my life.

Verse four of Psalm 139 says, 'Even before there is a word on my tongue, behold, O Lord, you know it all.' J.C. Philpot took the following approach to this verse:

> How needful it is to set a watch before the doors of our mouth, to hold that unruly member of ours, the tongue, as with bit and bridle. Some of you feel at times that you can scarcely say a word, and the less you say the better. Well, it may be as well; for great talkers are almost sure to make slips with their tongue.[7]

Certainly I am, and have been, guilty of using too many words.

Some nights I would descend the staircase from my children's rooms feeling like the worst mother: how could they possibly have settled to sleep on that low note! Many times I've had the eye-roll; the not-another-sermon whine; and the how-long's-this-sermon-going-to-take groan. I've even had 'I liked you better when you weren't a Christian!'

At times my children have been the sinful ones, at times it's been me and often it's been all three of us. Seeking forgiveness from children is a humbling experience. I recall very vividly when I started saying sorry to my children. Prior to this I did not believe for a moment that parents said sorry; as far as I was concerned parents were the ones in authority and apologising would totally undermine that authority! It really has been quite a journey of discovery and learning for me, but by the grace of God go I!

The last verse in this first section of Psalm 139 states: 'Such knowledge is too wonderful for me; it is too high, I cannot attain to it.' While we can learn about God through what He has revealed to us in the Bible, He *is* God and is way beyond our comprehension.

> 'For My thoughts are not your thoughts, nor are your ways My ways,' declares the LORD. 'For as the heavens are higher than the earth, so are My ways higher than your ways and My thoughts than your thoughts.' (Isaiah 55:8-9)

So we can be content to rest in the fact that God has revealed to us all the knowledge we need.

> 'The secret things belong to the LORD our God, but the

things revealed belong to us and to our sons forever, that we may observe all the words of this law.' (Deuteronomy 29:29)

I'll just slip in one final thought from Spurgeon whose writing on verse six is so poetic I simply cannot leave it out:

> Such knowledge not only surpasses my comprehension, but even my imagination. Mount as I may, this truth is too lofty for my mind. It seems to be always above me, even when I soar into the loftiest regions of spiritual thought. Is it not so with every attribute of God? Can we attain to any idea of His power, His wisdom, His holiness? Our mind has no line with which to measure the Infinite. Do we therefore question? Say, rather, that we therefore believe and adore. We are not surprised that the Most Glorious God should in his knowledge be high above all the knowledge to which we can attain: it must of necessity be so, since we are such poor limited beings; and when we stand a-tip-toe we cannot reach to the lowest step of the throne of the Eternal.[8]

Chapter 3

He is With Me

One of the hardest times in my life was when my dad died and, simply put, insomnia led to insanity. I want to share with you my journey in 2002 when I was diagnosed as having a brief psychotic episode. Initially they called it post-traumatic stress disorder.

My body went into shock the moment I got the phone call on 9 March 2002 informing me that my dad had died from a massive heart attack in the early hours of that morning. Now I understand many people experience this type of situation, many who may have been closer to their loved one than I was to my dad. So why this news triggered insomnia for me, I do not know. Was it because my last memory of Dad was an argument? Or because of the various drugs I had consumed over the previous 15 years? Or was it the marijuana in my system from the night before? Did those factors have anything to do with it? I don't know and I don't believe any person does know how the individual mind works in various scenarios. But what I do know is that from the day I got the news I spent the following ten nights without sleep.

Day one saw me and my family, my three siblings and their spouses, head straight to Mum in Levin. While staying the first night at the motels my parents owned, I stared at the ceiling hearing the odd train go through but I just couldn't 'shut down' to sleep. I was the only one of my siblings to have two toddlers with me over the time we were with Mum until after the funeral. In hindsight it would have been better to have arranged for them to stay with others as two days after arriving at Mum's I noticed my two-and-a-half-year-old son was missing.

I looked around the house and then noticed the gate leading outside had been opened slightly. Heading out, I rounded the top of the driveway to see my wee boy toddling into the middle of the road, some 15 metres in front of me. This was no quiet back street but a main road. It usually carried a heavy volume of cars and trucks, but on this particular mid-morning it was uncommonly quiet. As I ran towards my son I pleaded with him to come to me and was so relieved when his little body turned, ran and melted into my arms. In spite of the relief in that moment, seeing my son so vulnerable on the road felt like another wounding blow. That, mixed with two sleepless nights – I felt like I couldn't take any more!

On the day of the funeral I was full of angst but was able to 'keep it together'. I think there was a blowfly hovering because I became more fixated on blowflies over the following days as my mental state declined. This was Day Five of no sleeping and I was becoming hypersensitive to comments and nervy about movement. We went back to our home on a farm and it was not long before agoraphobia set in. This began with a fear of leaving the house and progressed to fear of leaving my bedroom. Sometimes I felt I was living my life through the eyes of a movie I had seen. For example, one night I had an argument with my husband and in my mind, our words were synonymous with those Demi Moore spoke to Rob Lowe in the movie *About Last*

Night. Another night I thought flowers that had been delivered were for my husband and children as I had died but was still in the home, just like the scenario from the Bruce Willis movie *The Sixth Sense*. My thinking was so irrational yet to me it was very real.

My worst memory was my final night before hospital: I was suicidal. I don't know if I actually had a knife in my hand but I do recall thinking it was going to be a messy death. Somehow, in the midst of it I wanted to choose God and not die. I remember kneeling – it was like a dream – I was receiving an accolade, I was about to be knighted. Bizarre I know, but I am fascinated looking back and reflecting on how my mind 'tripped'. My brother saw me around this time and he says it was like a switch went off and I was no longer there.

After being admitted to hospital, my brothers and mother came to visit but I was still 'gone'. I am so sad that my mother had this worry so soon after losing her husband; it was around this time she discovered a big lump in her stomach. The hospital told my family my condition had come on suddenly so I was likely to come out of it just as suddenly, which I did. It was quite an amazing morning; I remember sitting in the hospital courtyard watching the sunrise and I just knew I was okay and it was safe to start thinking about my dear dad. This may have been when God first started calling me, when He started drawing me to Himself. However, I cannot be sure of that, since the next few years would hold divorce and drunkenness.

I left the hospital medicated and on my first night home what did I do – smoke marijuana! Oddly enough when I went to the toilet, my mind tricked me into thinking I was going to get an anal probing while I sat there. Fortunately this swore me off marijuana for good. I remained on prescription medication for psychosis and anxiety but some weeks later I was on a bus to Mum's and I had an anxiety attack.

I thought my heart would pound out of my chest. I was sitting right behind the driver who was getting messages over his radio about a concerning individual. In my mind a criminal deviant was about to board our bus. I was freaking out. When I described this to the psychiatrist on returning home, he said it was my body naturally wanting to address anxiety and the medication was heightening the anxiety. I gradually weaned off all medication.

Five months later, I went through Mum's death without any drugs or alcohol. I was determined to sleep and not have a repeat of the psychosis. Fortunately there were no signs. I think I was quite numb those days and really sad. I found my comfort mostly in Tim Tams and Toffee Pops! For the next year I used herbal tablets if I found shutting down to sleep difficult. This was not often, but there was one really stressful occasion when I took one of my anti-psychosis tablets. But in reality alcohol became my self-medication for the next three and a half years.

I am curious and quite fascinated by the psychotic episode I had. When I was unwell, the night before I was admitted to the hospital, my brother said I was 'gone'. He also said I quoted Scripture accurately. I recall ranting away because, in my mind, I was Jesus or at least one of His apostles but my Bible knowledge was extremely limited, actually closer to non-existent. I cannot for one minute explain this. I had never read Scripture and while my brother had recited verses from the Bible over the week of Dad's death, they did not correlate to what I was saying in the hospital.

Fascinating! There is so much here to unpack and consider that I sincerely hope to research this field in much greater depth.

This is an area that, when talked about (rarely), it is often not in the context of God's word.

While I am delighted at how easy it was to quit smoking marijuana after my time at the psych unit, when I became a single parent the desire for alcohol grew stronger and stronger. By the time I was regularly attending a local church but had not yet made a commitment to follow Jesus, I was a binge drinker. When my children were staying with their dad, I would often be out drinking with friends. The year before the drinking stopped there were three separate occasions when, after a night of heavy drinking, I was really ill, and I mean *really* ill! In Chapter 1, I shared a journal entry dated 25 September 2005. Let me explain to you more of what happened that morning!

It was one of the three Sunday mornings where I was very ill. Unfortunately, I had told my study group I would share that morning at church about how our study was going. Throughout the morning, I battled over going for quite a few hours as I was so ill I couldn't even hold down water and Panadol. However, I had told my study group that I would speak and, since I like to think I was raised to have integrity, when I say I'll do something I like to keep my word.

So I dragged my sorry, smelly carcass to church to fulfil my obligation. I thought, *No big deal; I'll pop up when called, say my piece, and shrivel away into the back seat with task accomplished!* Well, it didn't happen like that. The worship leader made all the people who were sharing that morning sit in a row facing the congregation. I was seated between two of the most godly men in our church. Both were homeschooling, missionary men with solid views on raising families. I was sitting up there thinking, *I am getting my just desserts.* I was embarrassed as I knew they could smell alcohol on me. The embarrassment was mixed with self-pity as I couldn't believe I was in this situation. In addition there was a sense of shame – how could *I* even be speaking – and disgust at how could I share about a Holy God in my state. What a morning!

So much can be learnt when we mess up, can't it? I knew I did not want to stay in this state of self-loathing. But with hindsight this is exactly where I needed to be to see the true state of poor puny me. I welcome reminders of how wretched I was and can be because it highlights just how incredibly gracious, patient and forgiving God is.

Psalm 139:7-12 tells of God's omnipresence; He is everywhere:

> Where can I go from Your Spirit?
> Or where can I flee from Your presence?
> If I ascend to heaven, You are there;
> If I make my bed in Sheol, behold, You are there.
> If I take the wings of the dawn,
> If I dwell in the remotest part of the sea,
> Even there Your hand will lead me,
> And Your right hand will lay hold of me.
> If I say, 'Surely the darkness will overwhelm me,
> And the light around me will be night,'
> Even the darkness is not dark to You,
> And the night is as bright as the day.
> Darkness and light are alike to You.

When I read these verses, I think of how far away from God I have been. My life has been dark at times – doing heavy drugs, hanging out with heavy drinkers – fully engaged in self-destructive yet self-gratifying behaviour. The verses in this psalm tell me that God was always there and God saw it all.

Mental disorders are a controversial topic that is becoming more and more talked about in the media. I am totally fascinated as to how God, in His sovereignty, allowed this event in my life and why I now want to share about it. There is so much to unpack ... I would often cry when thinking or talking about it. It was big at the time. It carries a lot of painful, frustrating and disturbing memories. But I find that the more I talk and write about it, along with obtaining my notes from the hospital, the more I can come to terms with it.

Mental disorders is an area that most people really know little about. While some have staunch views, others have misinformed views. It is also a very sensitive area particularly to those who have experienced and more pointedly, still experience daily what is commonly known as mental illness. In sharing this experience, I sincerely hope it brings encouragement and hope to any reader struggling in this area, as well as awareness to those whose family members or friends are affected by this.

My heart is so full to see people free: free from guilt, shame, isolation, and darkness. 'Even the darkness is not dark to You, and the night is as bright as the day. Darkness and light are alike to You.' This verse from Psalm 139 points to the God of heaven and earth who is our hope, in whom we are to trust. He is much bigger than any experience, obstacle or thought that you have that even hints of being insurmountable. He is with us every step of the way. Are we holding on to Him? Are we surrendering all to Him? Do we really trust Him?

I am delighted to share in the next chapter how I surrendered to Him and found the way, the truth and the life (John 14:6).

Chapter 4

He Loves Me

I began studying for a certificate in counselling theory in the first year of my single-mum walk. While this enabled me to learn more about helping myself, I typically did not stick to the advice.

On 13 May 2006 my hard heart was transformed. It was a Saturday morning and I was home alone. No work to get up to, no children to attend to – the perfect morning to be drawn to my knees beside my bed and ask Jesus to be my Lord and Saviour. I acknowledged my life of sin, my sorrow for this and my desire to follow Him. I thanked Him for removing the debt of sin from my life by dying on the cross and rising again in victory over death. I then climbed back into bed and proceeded to read the Bible. I had started reading on 1 January of that year, more as a New Year's resolution than anything else! It was a memorable New Year morning as I was sandwiched between my two children in a tent at a camping site. We had joined with another family from our hometown and other friends they had invited from around the country. It had been an okay night. While the tent smelt just a little from my night's drinking, it wasn't too muggy to make a start on reading the Bible. So while the children slept I read, and I liked it. I looked forward to the next morning when I could read again, and the next.

What was funny is that come 13 May when I climbed back into bed and was reading from the gospel of John, I thought *Hang on I've read something like this before!* I flicked through the preceding gospels and sure enough they contained quite similar information! When I read the account of Mary visiting the tomb on the morning Jesus rose and assuming He was the gardener (John 20:15), I laughed out loud. I had the most amazing morning, laughing and crying over Scripture. Every Saturday morning, when the children were at their dad's, I would have hours of precious time, just me and God, immersed in His Word. Within a month of asking Jesus into my life I was baptised. It was a great day sharing my new faith and how I had come to be in God's family with others. The next day my children and I went to a Christian ranch. This would become a regular school holiday event for the next four years.

That first week after my baptism was something else! I felt like I was walking half a foot above the ground and people told me I was glowing. I must confess that before I entered a church I thought church people were dull. As a complete heathen, I had stereotyped Christians as people who wore brown, knitted vests and long socks with Roman sandals. My new church family was nothing like that stereotypical picture and those I met at the ranch were a group of fun-loving people. What impressed me most were the teenagers who chose to use their school holidays to be leaders for the children who attended. For one week, we would rise early and have an action-packed day of games, sport, devotions and free time. It was great and I soon got the role of Camp Mum. I often thought how much fun the leaders were having without any of the drugs and alcohol that had so easily enticed me. They had a freedom and a joy that I had no idea existed when I was their age. It made me sad for that teenage girl who lost her ambition and drive when drugs took centre stage.

I am so thankful for our time at the ranch. It gave me and the children great memories of school holiday fun that I would not have otherwise been able to afford. The highlight for me was horse riding, and a night walk through the bush complete with glow worms! God really spoilt us over this season of fun and joy and we all praised and worshipped Him in true camp style. A simple joy that came from going to camp was coming home. For that last weekend, before school got the monopoly on my children's time, we would 'camp out' in my room or on the lounge floor. We would watch movies and catch up on sleep. They were precious times and I was resting in His love for me.

In 2010 I was fortunate enough to be mentored by a lovely woman from my church (the same lady that gave me Angela Thomas' book). A question she asked me on our first day was, 'Who is Jo?' I didn't know where to start with this question so, seeing my struggle, she clarified, 'What does God want Jo to be?' It was still a difficult question for me but one I considered worthy of exploring more deeply. As I pondered, I came to see that my life had purpose and many opportunities. I came to identify the things in my life that made it full and satisfying. I could say I was a Christian woman, mother of two, social worker, friend and sister. There was more I could have added but I concluded that these were the things that defined who I am. I also concluded that these were my God-given responsibilities, and great blessings, and God wanted me to handle these well.

As I reflect on my journey I laugh at myself because of my regular 'pity-parties'. In the past I used alcohol to numb the pity I felt. It is so easy to make it all about self when there is no accountability to God. Once I became His child, I had a different view of my pity-party sessions. I viewed them much like the time when my toddler threw a temper tantrum at the supermarket. My tantrum could last up to two weeks (my toddler took only a few minutes!) and included not wanting to read, not wanting to parent, crying and using escapisms such as excessive movies and eating. I would be stewing over the unfairness of my situation. *I don't want to be single, life is too hard*, and *will anyone ever love me*.

I marvel at how God would gently shift my sight from me to Him, generally by the Spirit convicting, through another person or from His Word. My head would bow in shame as the realisation of my sin and inadequacy would weigh heavy on me in the light of His grace and mercy. If you can relate to this you know that the only way to find relief is through repentance.[1] As I reflect on five years as a Christian single mother, I thank God that the pity-parties reduced significantly in occurrence and severity.

Between 2011 and 2013, when I was a care and protection social worker, I worked closely with families for as long as a year with the hope of seeing change. Just like me earlier, these families seldom stuck with the advice we gave or the changes we tried to implement. There would generally be an initial enthusiasm to approach parenting or personal change from a new perspective, but it was often short-lived. I believe this is because we can easily fall back into unhealthy habits, including too much television, drugs or alcohol. At the root of it, I believe, is our natural selfishness. I cringe when I hear a mother say she isn't getting what she wants. The words haunt me as they mirror how I used to view my life. Unfortunately, this blind state creates an unhappy, unfulfilled life of loathing. Selfishness makes it all about self and then loneliness waltzes in because there is little room for thinking of others. I recall that as a young person I thought my parents were zapped onto this earth as adults to take care of me. I gave no thought to their marriage, mortgage, bills and responsibilities; it was all about me! This is generally how children think. So when the only adult in the home is behaving in the same way, it tends not to go so well.

> For You formed my inward parts;
> You wove me in my mother's womb.
> I will give thanks to You, for I am fearfully and wonderfully made;
> Wonderful are Your works,
> And my soul knows it very well.
> My frame was not hidden from You,
> When I was made in secret,
> And skilfully wrought in the depths of the earth;
> Your eyes have seen my unformed substance;
> And in Your book were all written
> The days that were ordained for me,
> When as yet there was not one of them.
>
> How precious also are Your thoughts to me, O God!
> How vast is the sum of them!
> If I should count them, they would outnumber the sand.
> When I awake, I am still with You. (Psalm 139:13-18)

This to me is the climax of the entire psalm. When I studied the words intently, I learnt so much, particularly verses 13 and 14. Because God made me, this really helped me to understand better who I am. It was a light-bulb moment that rested on the six words, 'I will give thanks to You.' I see the words 'You wove me in my mother's womb' and 'I am fearfully and wonderfully made', as connected only when I give thanks to the One who created me. The incredible weaving of our being from the day of conception is all God's work. Spurgeon calls the womb where it takes place 'the secret workshop.'[2] When, and only when, we give thanks to Him for our creation can we truly see how fearfully and wonderfully He has made us to be. These words, so beautifully written conveying so much love, ascend to 'my soul knows it very well'. Wow! This is love and contentment that goes right to the soul. Right where no one but our amazing God can penetrate.

I believe loneliness is a hindrance to the wellness of our soul. This is especially relevant to single mums and is an area that God worked on in my life. For me, loneliness was defeated by the reality that He loves me. We can combat loneliness with a grateful, full life that trusts in the saving and transforming power of Jesus Christ, regardless of our circumstances (2 Thessalonians 3:16). When loneliness occupies the single mum, the next visitor can be fear. This is when things can go from bad to worse creating more distance in the parent-child relationship. Fears can spring from thoughts such as:

- my child loves their dad more,
- my child loves their stepmother more,
- my child does not enjoy being with me,
- the grief and pain from the death of my child's dad will never heal, and
- my child has so much to deal with I cannot discipline them.

There are myriads of fears, but there is one solution: love. When we have certainty that God loves us, we do not fear (1 John 4:18-19). When we have certainty that His Word is truth, we do not fear. When we know what is written in His Word is for His glory and our good, then we do not fear. Love will conquer any fears of inadequacy when we allow God to pour His truth into us. His truth will overflow from us to our children and into our other relationships. God's Word has an abundance of promises of eternal life (John 3:16). For example, when a Christian parent dies, fear can be overcome by holding fast to the promise of heaven.

I love listening to David Crowder's music; he is a talented musician whose songs are great worship to God. One song in particular contains the words 'there is nothing on earth that heaven can't heal'.

However, there is an individual responsibility as a godly mother to be filled with God's Word; without the Word believers become spiritually weak. We must be in His Word. We should be prayerfully addressing our problems and being supported by strong Christian believers to help us overcome any fears causing distance with our children.

Women can feel abandoned at the time of separation from their children's father. It is easy to feel completely let down by men, be it an absent father (literally or emotionally), rejection by boyfriends or memories of arguments. Divorce becomes the grand finale! Separation from a spouse, whether through death or divorce, is a time when our world caves in and we gasp for breath. Abandonment can also come from those people who you expected to be a support. It is said there is no guarantee of receiving quality support from the church. Why is that? Why is it that in our time of desperate need, quality support can sometimes be hard to find? Seeds of bitterness and rejection can grow into isolation and anger which are dangerous for both mother and child. Possibly support is wanting because of a mix of hurt and pride on the part of the mother and inadequacy of understanding on the part of supporters.

Sometimes it is easier to give than to receive. I enjoy receiving and God is showing me humility in receiving graciously but all too often pride has reigned. I would tell people I was fine and then grumble to myself about the lack of support I got. My lawns would be a good example. With study, work and children I would sometimes have a long-stemmed paddock out back and question why the church folk weren't coming to my aid. But not only did I not ask, but it was a rear section. No one could even *see* my lawns let alone know they were overgrown!

Kiwis can be terrible at asking for help – the old stiff upper lip concept is still entrenched in our society! Then we complain about a lack of assistance when we have not actually asked for any. But there are times we have stepped out and the support has been inadequate. Some people can make thoughtless comments. One person described their experience as leaving them thinking that 'people mean well but they can end up being mean!' I know I have been guilty on more than one occasion of speaking before thinking.

There are a few experiences in life that, unless you have been through them, you really have no idea how they can affect a person. There are days when all is well with the soul and others where anything anyone says is going to produce tears or a stone-face. Sometimes a hug with no words is beneficial. Listening can be more important than talking. Prayer is always helpful and sharing a prayerful verse can make a difference. Please don't get me wrong, I know only too well there is a huge number of

Christians and non-Christians who give wonderful support and aid to those in need.

I have been blessed to have some counselling opportunities with a few lovely ladies. I love encouraging others in their walk with Jesus. When I work with people whose lives have become complex, or feel that way, I like to keep counsel simple. Often I address their issues of concern; establish a reading plan in God's Word; and then support them in a discipling relationship. Strengthening Christians in Jesus is more important than any worldly philosophy or being dependent on anyone or any vice. God turns our experiences to good regardless of how hurtful they are at the time; they provide us with an opportunity to grow more like Jesus (Romans 8:28-29). Jerry Bridges states this when writing about anger:

> I have found that a firm belief in the sovereignty of God is my first defence against a temptation to allow anger to linger in my mind and emotions. If I want to deal with the temptation decisively, I actively call to my mind that the actions of another person (or persons) that triggered my initial response of anger are under the sovereign control of God. Though the actions may be sinful in themselves, God intends them for my good. As Joseph said to his brothers, 'As for you, you meant evil against me, but God meant it for good' (Genesis 50:20). As I have already observed, the good may be an opportunity to grow in Christlikeness. But God may also have other ends in view, perhaps to prepare us in some way for greater usefulness. Or we may never know what good God brought out of a specific situation where we were tempted to become angry.[3]

Cries of 'I don't deserve this hardship', 'I don't understand this' and 'I don't want it' will not take the hurt away. Time does heal when we attend to our wounds under the counsel of our great Physician. These wounds will continue to remain open or become a scar depending on how much is surrendered. Prior to becoming a Christian the counsel I received summed up my wounds with the word *rejection*. This coincided with my thinking and justified me in adopting a victim mentality rather than an awareness of my sins. Coming to Christ as a sinner was fundamentally important. Had I come as a victim I might have missed the point and not seen Christ as my saviour through victory over sin. The danger was that I could have viewed Christ as a victim, rejected and the only one who understood me. This perspective is not incorrect, but what is incorrect is not seeing myself as a sinner.

We cannot have an accurate view of God and His grace until we have an accurate view of self and our inner rottenness. We are not deserving of anything – Jesus took our punishment in our place when, rightfully, God could send us all to hell as guilty sinners (Romans 5:6-8). It is grace alone that saves us (Ephesians 2:8; 2 Timothy 1:9) and until we truly understand our sin nature, we will not understand God's grace and mercy towards us. When a person becomes His child, so much is gained. We have freedom from the bondages of rejection, bitterness, confusion and loneliness.

There is no one on the planet who can promise never to leave you. Jesus is the only one who can make that promise – *He will never leave you* (Hebrews 13:5). We must rest in that. I pray this truth will bring you comfort on those hard days.

Earlier, I shared that I had become more aware of my self-pity parties and how to view and manage them. I would be convicted of the need to repent of focusing on self and turn my focus to pleasing God. The chart below[4] is an excellent resource to show the difference between God leading us to conviction versus experiencing condemnation for unrepented sin:

Conviction versus Condemnation

Conviction from God	*Condemnation from Satan*
Pinpoints problems	Obscures problems
Targets specific actions	Makes general accusations
Leads to repentance (godly sorrow)	Leads to regret (worldly sorrow)
Offers solutions	Appoints blame
Makes us hopeful	Makes us hopeless
Enables us to change	Keeps us from change
Brings us closer to God	Drives us away from God

Warning: What starts as conviction by the Holy Spirit can quickly turn to condemnation from the enemy if we don't respond immediately with repentance. Be quick to obey and don't grieve the Holy Spirit, for He desires to help you.

> Blessed are they whose transgressions are forgiven,
> whose sins are covered. (Romans 4:7)

We are continually learning about who we are in Christ. Being a Christian is all about changing to be more like Christ and growth occurs when we put off self and put on Christ (Ephesians 4:22-24). Consider where you are strong and where weakness lies. For example, I love to read and be busy seeing people. I get a lot of joy interacting with people but I also need time alone. I generally serve in small doses as I tend to migrate to talking. I will be the annoying one who is chatting away while others are busy packing up!

Serving others helps reduce self-pitying thoughts. Serving gives us motivation and opportunity for connecting with others while taking our eyes off ourselves. We can use what we enjoy doing with other people – for example, music, art, home decorating, cooking, or entertaining. If you are a musician, you could visit some of the older members of your church and play for them. If you cook, find families that would appreciate a home-cooked meal or baking. This does require reaching out and talking to people which I know a number of women find difficult. (I will discuss ideas for communication in Chapter 7). Where possible, your children should be right beside you when you are serving.

Indicators of being involved with too much serving can include being irritated too easily with the children, having an untidy house, and becoming overtired. Indicators of not serving enough may include boredom, a lack of joy and dwelling on wrong thinking. The way to find balance is to ensure you are having quality time each day with God while maintaining your responsibilities. Quality time to pray and soak in Scripture. Then what God pours into you will overflow to others.

There are a few verses that speak about being a good steward – for example, Luke 12:41-43 and 1 Peter 4:10. But Matthew chapter 25 is perhaps the most important. The only words I long to hear from my Master are, 'Well done good and faithful servant.' It is good to spend some time thinking about who we are and what responsibilities God has entrusted to us. Are you struggling with responsibilities or giving them your best?

One study I like to do with others has a line that I enjoy recalling. 'Our responsibility is to be faithful in the present; God takes care of the results in the present and future.'[5] Rest and relax in the fact that God is responsible for the results of each day, for our future and our children's future. We are simply required to faithfully follow Him. What does faithfully following Him mean? I believe we can look to the two main commandments in the New Testament: 'You shall love the Lord your God with all your heart, and with all your soul, and with all your strength, and with all your mind; and your neighbour as yourself' (Matthew 22:37; Luke 10:27). Therefore as we seek to be loving to others we must do so without compromising our first love for God. It is our love for God that motivates our actions, words and thoughts. However, we need to guard ourselves against pleasing others versus loving others, including our children and family. It can happen as subtly as allowing children to get their own way rather than obeying you.

> People often erroneously begin by letting children have their own way, letting them avoid responsibility, focusing on following their feelings, and then, later endeavour to do just the opposite at some point in the child's growth. This confusing double standard is unbiblical.[6]

This is such an easy trap. When we seek to please, rather than love, our children or others we risk getting disgruntled and frustrated. We can spiral into loneliness as we pull away from these relationships. Distance in our relationships needs to be overcome, especially in our relationships with our children.

Before turning to the next chapter on God's protection, here are some Bible verses to meditate on:

> Brethren, I do not regard myself as having laid hold of it yet; but one thing I do: forgetting what lies behind and reaching forward to what lies ahead. (Philippians 3:13)

> Therefore be imitators of God, as beloved children; and walk in love, just as Christ also loved you and gave Himself up for us, an offering and a sacrifice to God as a fragrant aroma. (Ephesians 5:1-2)

> If possible, so far as it depends on you, be at peace with all men. (Romans 12:18)

Chapter 5

He Protects Me

When you first hand over your children for access, the emotional trauma can be huge. Following many hand-overs I cried the whole way home and always felt like my arms were missing. I still recall the very first time. It was a dark rainy Friday night and all of me wanted to call it off. We met halfway and it was just over three hours between homes. We did this virtually every fortnight for seven years.

Routine access between parents, no matter how difficult, is very important for settling into life as a split family. Initially my children's father would pop in whenever he could as he had long, messy farming hours. This was unsettling for all of us. When he left farming and was no longer working weekends we set up the fortnightly weekend access and within a short space of time we saw the benefits. I could plan my weekends and the children knew whether they could attend a birthday party. I saw a change in their dad after about six months. He settled into planning things for his weekend with the children and really delighted in having them. Consistency has always been a battle for me and, true to form, no sooner had the fortnightly access been established I tried to shift and move dates around to fit in with other events. Fortunately, their father did not budge, reminding me of the need to stick to our dates regardless.

As time went on we came to have flexibility for certain situations but overall we never missed our fortnightly weekend access. My children were okay telling friends they couldn't make their birthday party as they were with their dad. The relationship between child and father is more important than friends and cake! Other activities were sacrificed as well such as weekend sport and church. It was sad my children didn't have consistency each weekend with their sport teams (I don't think we were ever the coach's favourites) as their father was three hours away from our home. However, this all changed when my eldest started college and I relocated to the same region as their dad. After seven years of fortnightly travel, meeting halfway on the Friday night and the Sunday afternoon, I can say not one of us regret doing it. We can also say how excellent it was once the long distance travel stopped.

I learnt early that I did not have it together to make my marriage work so I couldn't expect separated parenting would be any easier. However, I soon learnt that if we, the parents, work hard at it for the children's sake, we may find a mature friendship forms. And I am pleased to say that thirteen years later my children's dad and I are supportive friends to each other and our families. I would even say he is family to me.

I recall one access visit when we had an argument during his hand-over to me. I wasn't getting my own way on the subject of where the children should one day go to college. As I drove home I was raging and thinking, *He is getting the 'cold shoulder' for the next ten years, I'll only discuss necessary stuff and there'll be no pleasantries*. Within 24 hours I sent him a text apologising! This was way out of character for me; he was used to the silent treatment which was my usual response. I had become a Christian and the old self was being replaced by the new self.

(Please read Appendix B for a perspective on shared access from a father. Appendix C gives New Zealand legal information regarding access and includes resources available for support.)

The first single parent mentioned in the Bible is Hagar, an Egyptian slave around 2165-1990 BC.[1] Hagar was the slave of Abram's wife Sarai (later known as Abraham and Sarah). After ten years of waiting for God's promise to give them a child, Sarai was desperate and asked Abram to conceive a child with Hagar (Genesis 16:2-4). However, when she fell pregnant Hagar despised Sarai and fled when Sarai dealt harshly with her. God found Hagar in the wilderness and told her to return to her duty and to submit to Sarai. When her son Ishmael became a teenager, he mocked the household and this time Hagar was sent away. In the wilderness, Hagar was convinced Ishmael would die of thirst but again God came to her aid. God restored Hagar and was with her and Ishmael as they lived out their lives in the wilderness of Egypt (Genesis 21:16-20).

There is much to learn from Hagar's story but the point I want to focus on is how God protected Hagar and how we can draw on that same protection for our parenting. This story can encourage single parents today, some four thousand years later. At times, we may feel we are wandering in lonely places where danger and uncertainty lurk. As God's children, we are never alone.[2] Hagar called God *El ro'i'* (Genesis 16:13) which is Hebrew for 'God sees'. The giving of this name 'arose from her astonishment at having been the object of God's gracious attention'.[3] God protected Hagar while she was pregnant in the wilderness by sending her back to a household that worshipped Him. The second time Hagar was in the wilderness God protected her and kept Ishmael from dying of thirst. We can rest also in His protection and in the many promises of His Word as He will honour every single one. This leads us to the last section of Psalm 139:

> O that You would slay the wicked, O God;
> Depart from me, therefore, men of bloodshed.
> For they speak against You wickedly,
> And Your enemies take Your name in vain.
> Do I not hate those who hate You, O LORD?
> And do I not loathe those who rise up against You?
> I hate them with the utmost hatred;
> They have become my enemies.
> Search me, O God, and know my heart;
> Try me and know my anxious thoughts;
> And see if there be any hurtful way in me,
> And lead me in the everlasting way. (Psalm 139:19-24)

The beginning of these verses highlights our need to stay clear of wicked people, those who reject God. We need to avoid any close association with them. Leupold adds:

> Thus the concluding verse offers the thought, if there is anything that is in the least unwholesome, may God help him to see it, remove it, and walk in the way of life, which is the 'way everlasting', and keep him from 'every way that leads to pain', which is, of course, the way of sin.[4]

I recall times of feeling very vulnerable as a single mum, battling for my family against the attacks that came both from within and externally. Protection is needed for our own personal walk with the Lord as we make our way in the world. As a single Christian woman you are the spiritual leader in the home so the devil will seek to attack and overwhelm you and render you ineffective: 'Be of sober *spirit,* be on the alert. Your adversary, the devil, walks about like a roaring lion, seeking someone he may devour' (1 Peter 5:8). Be on guard and protect your family. We need to be aware not only of the associations we and our children are keeping but also the influence of television and social media. I have seen too many women looking for 'Mr Right' on chatrooms and dating sites, only to find more heartache and problems.

Consider the following verse: 'For among them are those who enter into households and captivate weak women weighed down with sins, led on by various impulses, always learning and never able to come to the knowledge of the truth' (2 Timothy 3:6-7). While the Lord offers us protection against the many attacks that can come against our families, we have an important role. We must be wise about the male company we keep. We need to remain under God's protection by not wilfully sinning or remaining in sin but rather through an obedient life:

> Behold, the LORD's hand is not so short that it cannot save; nor is His ear so dull that it cannot hear. But your iniquities have made a separation between you and your God, and your sins have hidden His face from you so that He does not hear. (Isaiah 59:1-2)

Jesus says, 'if you love me you will obey Me' (John 14:15). Consider also, 'But resist him [the devil], firm in *your* faith, knowing that the same experiences of suffering are being accomplished by your brethren who are in the world' (1 Peter 5:9).

You are not alone in the fight. To help us resist and stand firm we will look at four aspects of parenting: consistency, communication, change and creativity. They are spiritual disciplines that can be God's means of protection.

Consistency

> How blessed are those whose way is blameless, who walk in the law of the Lord. (Psalm 119:1)

Good living habits strengthen us for the daily battles as well as the unexpected. Consistent routines help keep the family on task and aware of what is expected of them. They also help to see when there is opportunity for rest. Routines are essential for night-time when children are young. The danger of sending children off to sleep at irregular hours after watching lots of television, playing computer games or after yelling at them, may mean they lie awake for hours. Their brain may be so hyped up they can't sleep. This is not a good pattern to be in! Sleep routine ideally starts from birth. Beware of quick solutions. We can resort to them for 'peace' in the moment but they often have long-term paybacks. Sometimes it will take two hard weeks (or more) to break a habit but it will be well worth it.

If bedtime is difficult with your young one, then try sticking to a routine like this, for example: bath or shower, into pyjamas, read a story in bed, pray and talk, leave. As your child grows they can read you their story in bed but always try to have that prayer and talk time. This may be the only time when you learn how their day was. If we say we are too tired to spend this time with our child then we may well find this time of day quickly becomes more exhausting, dramatic and, potentially, more argumentative. When your child is old enough you may have the odd night where you put yourself to bed first because you are so exhausted. While they are too young for that, a quick bedtime routine can suffice before you fall into your bed. Working hard at keeping our children in settled routines definitely pays off in the long run. Beware of traps such as needing 'my time' before the children are settled into bed. This tends to consist of watching television or time on the computer. The risk is when children feel second best there is a danger they may become resentful at the lack of attention and sooner or later rebel against this.

I would like to encourage you to consider studying in the evenings. It can be a long difficult journey, I know. I could easily have sat in front of the television each night when the children had gone to bed. But I will never regret studying. Learning is a gift, I did not waste my time and there have been many rewards. Have a look at what is available at learning institutes and universities; look at what is available part-time and by distance learning. Consider prayerfully and carefully how studying can fit in your family structure. Perhaps you could fulfil that dream you've always had.

Discipline was an area I found difficult to be consistent in. For example, one day there may be a consequence for a wrong action which is overlooked a couple of days later! However, just as God has graciously given us a book outlining His standards for our good, so must we endeavour to give clear and concise instructions to our children and stick with them. Sticking to them is the important part and Jay Adams covers this well:

> When a parent fails to police rules, he teaches that he doesn't mean business. He teaches that he is undependable. Some rules he may enforce sometimes (usually when

> he's had it), but no one ever can guess which or when. That is a shaky situation for a kid. He never knows when the hammer will fall.
>
> Once you have made a rule, every time that rule is broken you should know it and you should follow through with the stated penalty. When you make twenty-five or thirty rules, you must spend the whole day investigating to see if the rules are being broken. You won't have time for anything else. But if you make three (or better, two) rules and faithfully police them, it won't be very long before your children get the right idea. They will know that when a rule is made it is going to be followed up.[5]

Communication

> You shall love the LORD your God with all your heart and with all your soul and with all your might. These words, which I am commanding you today, shall be on your heart. You shall teach them diligently to your sons and shall talk of them when you sit in your house and when you walk by the way and when you lie down and when you rise up. (Deuteronomy 6:5-7)

You will notice that throughout this book I continually talk about the necessity of reading. As a further comment on the bedtime routine of reading, I want to draw your attention to the many benefits of consistently reading and teaching your children about God. Not only are we commanded to read and teach God's Word (Deuteronomy 4:9, 6:7; Joshua 1:8; Psalm 25:5, 119:15-16,35; Ephesians 6:4) but many biblically-based books can be a huge help in our parenting. Obedience to this command has many benefits: it encourages children to delight in reading; imparts valuable skills and knowledge for life and daily living; and both parent and child receive the same teachings. And as a single parent you have the benefit of a 'third person' rather that your continual teaching. That third person can back up what you have been saying for months! And when that third person is God you can always say, 'If you don't like it, take it up with God – He said it!' Often I would delight in how well authors would articulate teaching that I would fumble to say in any logical form.

Communication is such a big factor in our relationships. Psalm 139:20-21 describes how God's enemies speak about Him and the psalmist says, 'have nothing to do with them.'

When we are communicating the truth and promises of God to our children, we are giving them protection against the outside influences of this world (Proverbs 5:23, 10:17; Job 36:12). We are protecting them against the lies and unkind words that are rampant in our society. The Bible's book of Proverbs is full of moral wisdom and has much to say about communication. The purpose of the book is to cause people

> to know wisdom and instruction, to discern the sayings of understanding, to receive instruction in wise behaviour, righteousness, justice and equity; to give prudence to the naïve, to the youth knowledge and discretion, a wise man will hear and increase in learning, and a man of understanding will acquire wise counsel, to understand a proverb and a figure, the words of the wise and their riddles. The fear of the Lord is the beginning of knowledge; fools despise wisdom and instruction. (Proverbs 1:2-7)

Paul Tripp uses Proverbs 20:5 to draw out the heart of your teenager. He suggests asking open-ended questions to help your child communicate what he really thinks and really wants. Tripp suggests asking what he wants to do and why; what is important in the situation; what he fears the most; what would really make him happy; and what does he think God thinks about the circumstance? Tripp states that we don't need to harshly lecture someone who is open, communicative and teachable.[6]

One very important area of communication is in regard to the separated parents and how mums talk about their children's father. A lot of separations and divorces cause a continual battle between parents and the biggest loser is always the children. If you are caught in vicious battles (with anyone for that matter) then consider putting off the first half of this proverb and replacing it with the second half:

> There is one who speaks rashly like the thrusts of a sword, but the tongue of the wise brings healing. (Proverbs 12:18)

And Psalm 19:14 says,

> Let the words of my mouth and the meditation of my heart be acceptable in Your sight, O LORD, my rock and my Redeemer.

Can I encourage you to look to the future and remember that you are in the job of equipping your child to live in the world? I strongly recommend you don't run down marriage, if yours failed. Make a point of talking to your children regularly about when they find that special someone, get married and how they might be as parents. When our child shares with us the difficulty or unfairness of not having a dad around, use this as an opportunity to talk openly. Remind them that one day, Lord willing, they will be a parent and they can choose to do things differently.

Often Dad is in full-time work and so may be in the position to afford 'neat stuff' – the designer labels and expensive toys – while mum struggles to meet the monthly power bill and is still wearing her maternity bra when celebrating their child's eighth birthday! Don't be deluded by this, even if your children may appear to be. The most important ingredient that our children need from us is love, given in the form of time. This includes assisting with their emotional needs and not just their material needs. Be in the moment with your children: talk with them, listen to them, enjoy them – make them feel you do not want to be anywhere else in the world but right beside them. You are hearing about how the ball hit them in the face at school or how the teacher said their item of schoolwork was great and they read it out to the whole class. Regardless of how great or *stink* their dad is, you are their mum and where possible, you simply need to give them your best.

Forgiveness is a very important ingredient for stopping the raging battles. When separation occurs, emotions are raw and the first six months or so can be really vicious (I've talked with mums who are still at this stage, years down the track). Some accusations may be factual but they are often made just to hurt the other person in the same way they have hurt us. At times, not responding can be the best way to deal with things.

As a social worker I observed that many adults are not able to let anything go. There is one battle after another, sometimes through the courts and mostly ending up in a lose-lose situation.

When strong emotions are involved, words and decisions can be blurred and thoughtless creating more hurt and drama. Some family situations become hugely dramatic as a distraction from facing an issue head-on and dealing with it.

Sometimes it's not about 'having it out' with the other party – sometimes it is about forgiving people for the wrongs they have done, just as we hope people will forgive us for the wrongs we have done (Luke 11:4) and just as God has forgiven our sins (Matthew 18:21-35). As a parent we shouldn't be carrying an extra weight of bitterness and anger. Think about the times you have had something weighing on your mind and your child is beside you tugging on your shirt and you don't even register it is happening. As the adult you have to take responsibility for your bitterness and anger and sort through it.

As I shared earlier, I experienced a change in seeking forgiveness rather than dishing out the silent treatment as a consequence of not getting my own way. As a new Christian this change of attitude showed me God was working in my life, that He was changing me. God used Romans 12:18 to challenge my stubbornness: 'If possible, so far as it depends on you, be at peace with all men.' This verse can be applied to a number of relationships.

There can be great blessing when we learn to communicate well with others. When we do this in obedience to God's Word, much peace and harmony can result. A harmonious home is going to help in having settled children more so than a home full of angry and harsh words. When we are wrestling with turmoil in our lives it's easy to become angry. It is so important to deal with turmoil quickly so peace and harmony can return. My early childhood years were harmonious but once my older siblings reached their mid-teens my father struggled with his anger. There were several years when we lived with either yelling matches or the silent treatment. Work at having a home full of grace and harmony. Perhaps think through your issues when the children are in bed or let them go, forgive and move on. When your children are with you, aim to give them as much attention as possible. Never talk poorly of their father, and be 'in the moment' because you won't get that moment back.

One important component of communication is being able to share how we are feeling. I have often wondered whether the inability to communicate feelings could be due to one of the following:

- Denial – if I ignore the feelings they will go away
- Fear – if I discuss feelings it may make someone angry, feel burdened or reject me
- Unacceptable – reason and logic are preferred to emotions
- Untrained – not trained or experienced in expressing emotions
- Two-way – if I share my feelings they might share theirs and then I'd be uncomfortable.

It is important to understand that feelings are involuntary. Feelings are caused indirectly, not directly; they are indicators, not instigators. In and of themselves, feelings are not sin. How we deal with feelings can be sinful but nowhere in Scripture are we commanded to change our feelings. God only commands us to change our deeds – our thoughts, words and actions.[7]

How you respond to others, how you behave in your relationships in the home and outside of it is either going to be self-orientated or God-orientated. Self-orientated behaviour means you seek to please self and may hide behind one of the five styles above or some other self-protective way. If you seek to be God-orientated in your relationships, you will desire to please Him in your responses, regardless of how you feel. You will seek to be at peace with all people where possible and you will seek to learn to love and pray for even your enemies (Matthew 5:44).

> The most important training that children (as well as others we disciple) can receive is how to demonstrate love toward God and others (i.e. how to be a loving person). Biblical love is often difficult since it goes against the flesh; however, helping children be loving in the midst of difficulties is crucial. Therefore, parents should not necessarily take children out of difficult situations, but rather, help them to have victory in the midst of difficulties. It may be God's will that they learn important biblical lessons by staying in the situation. It is important to note that children tend not to remember what they are taught in a classroom setting nearly as well as truths they learn through experience, particularly when they are confronted with difficulties. When they are in the midst of difficult situations, children are much more attentive to instruction.[8]

Change

> Trust in the Lord with all your heart and do not lean on your own understanding. In all your ways acknowledge Him, and He will make your paths straight. (Proverbs 3:5-6)

There are two areas of change in our parenting: adjusting to life as a single-parent family, and our own maturity. God wants us to change and 'He who began a good work in you will perfect it until the day of Christ Jesus' (Philippians 1:6). We are to put off our old sinful ways and replace them with right living that pleases God.

> Turn your eyes upon Jesus,
> Look full in His wonderful face,
> And the things of earth will grow strangely dim
> In the light of His glory and grace.[9]

The words of this well-known hymn say it all. In times when single-mum friends have called me to say they just can't cope with what's going on, I will often remind them of the words of this hymn. All too often our tendency is to magnify the situation and forget that Jesus is there. But we need to meditate on these words when we are struggling with the changes that divorce can bring or with our role as a single parent. Let the words of this hymn shift your heart so you can see more clearly to deal with the temporary things of this world while awaiting the great reward of heaven.

When I struggled with change such as handing my children over for access, one approach that helped put the issue into perspective was putting my feet in their dad's shoes. If I found every second weekend difficult without my children, what must 12 days out of every 14 feel like for him? It helped to not discount his feelings. The effort required to maintain access can add a financial and other burdens, such as motivation and time management. It was costly for me to run my car to do two trips that took two hours each time every fortnight for seven years.

And there were times I really couldn't be bothered. What I soon came to realise was that the effort to maintain access conferred many benefits. It is very important that our children have the best opportunity to have a relationship with their father. Some mothers will say, 'You don't know how difficult he is ... he does this and that, and then this!' I urge you to be really careful here and not deny their dad visitation rights because you don't like him. I've already addressed this under communication but in terms of all the change a split family experiences, settling into routine access can be a great benefit both in the present and for the future. I sincerely would not like your children to turn eighteen and want nothing to do with you because they blame you for denying them their father. I have seen this happen on more than one occasion with children as young as fourteen.

Some fathers choose not to be in their children's lives. A young man shared with me how his father relocated to Australia when his parents separated in his childhood. He reflected upon his uncle as an important male figure who would hang out with him and his brother, take them hunting and fishing. He also recalled their church community was a place he could look up to the older men as an example of how to raise families and be men of faith. He reflected upon these examples as shaping him to be the young man he is today. He feels that without good examples a boy may otherwise question the importance of family, have an unhealthy view of right and wrong and lack authority and discipline. He also recalls his uncle being there to have the man talks when his brother was behaving poorly for his mother.

Creativity

As a single mother I have found the protection of God is

immense. I remember thinking, *How sad it is there isn't a dad in our home but the right Father has made His presence known to the very corners of each room*. God protects us in ways we can't even comprehend if we put our faith in Him. How much easier to fall asleep at night thinking about our heavenly Father folding his arms around us, holding us near. Psalm 34:18 says, 'The LORD is near to the brokenhearted, and saves those who are crushed in spirit.'

There are many areas in our lives where we need to walk by faith in His protection. I don't know about you, but I found in my single-parent walk there were seasons of little money or no money. Creativity was a necessity. I have always been sad when mothers talk about needing to work long hours for the money and struggling with afterschool and holiday care. As in every other area of life, God is not apart from us in this. I hope you can step out in faith and put hedges around your family's life. I discovered we did not end up on the streets when I made a stand not to work during school holidays. Perhaps you could work half the holidays if the children's dad or family are able to look after your children. Holiday breaks are not only important times for change from school routine, they are also essential for everyone to recharge – to break from the normal routine and have some really kick-back, relaxing days.

Even when finances are tight, an absolute must is to pay bills first – like housework, they never go away! Even paying a little each week will lighten the load. Perhaps you could write out a simple budget, clearly showing how much comes in each week and how much goes out. Don't compete with your children's father. Typically, he will be in a position to work a full week and get a decent salary which he may choose to lavish on your children. Celebrate this. Be careful not to think that your children will love him more for it. Children may well state how they love all they get from Dad, but don't equate this with a lack from you if you are busy meeting their day-to-day needs. Giving your children the warmth and security in the home is far more necessary and rewarding than the latest iPod or Nerf gun.

Flexibility and creativity are sometimes necessary to address struggles your child may be experiencing. For example, if your child is having a tough time getting to sleep, both the hall light and a bedside lamp may need to stay on or a radio/CD may need to be playing. You can simply switch these off when you go to bed. Roll with the needs for the moment until your normal routine falls back into place. Don't resist your child's requests but rather help and guide them to where they need to go.

If they have watched a scary movie at Dad's or at a cousin's home don't put that person's home down. Rather, remind your child they could have left the room and done something else or asked if they could watch a different movie. Any consequences from the child's inability to say 'no' to something scary or wrong can be an opportunity for you to guide them through that – but don't put the blame onto someone else. Keep healthy, open communication so they don't feel they are getting the other parent or person into trouble. You may need to spend extra time helping them get back into their sleep patterns but if you go about this gently your children learn to adapt. All too often I have heard mothers say, 'It takes days to get them settled again after being at their father's; it's just not worth it.' Actually it *is* worth it; unless they are at serious risk of abuse it is worth you giving quality time to helping it succeed.

I feel it is important to emphasise that you can help by holding back on negative comments about their dad. His choice of partner and lifestyle are common areas of criticism. Help children by teaching them what is right rather than on stressing what is wrong. God, by His grace, can help you to be an example, someone who makes your home a castle they feel safe in. If you don't feel you are a good example, or consider your home safe and welcoming then you can do something about it. (I will cover more on this in Chapter 7).

Guard your family in regard to who you talk to about your situation. For example, consider getting advice from a single parent whose home operates in harmony versus someone battling their children's father through the courts. Learn from a trusted source if you are concerned about things the children are exposed to at their fathers. Check you are not being oversensitive or hypocritical by allowing something you condemn their father for to occur in your own home. Take an honest look at yourself and prayerfully consider any areas you need to address which may be burdening you and your family.

The goal for our family is to please God and glorify Him with our lives. Wisdom and strength to protect our children and raise them in the fear and admonition of the Lord come from an obedient life. Settle into regular routines, let communication flow easily, address change creatively and simply so your children are not averse to it. Let peace and harmony symbolise your home and watch God guide and protect you in a way only He can.

Chapter 6

He Teaches Me

I have often heard people say they struggle to read God's Word. It seems most of us need some sort of reading plan to systematically work our way through the 66 books. For me it started with *The Word for Today*. This booklet has an informative, motivational paragraph followed by some 'soul food' i.e. scriptures to follow daily. I utilised this tool for the first two years of my walk before I thought, *I'm going to go it alone, just me and my Bible!* Just as I had decided to do this one of the elders announced that our church was going to be doing *The Bible in One Year* programme. This study collates an Old Testament chapter, a New Testament chapter, a Psalm and one chapter of Proverbs as well as a motivational paragraph for each day. So that was me for the next year. Once it finished I again thought, *Right I'm going it alone with just me and my Bible!* I struggled! I decided I wasn't ready to remove the trainer wheels so back came *The Word for Today* booklet. Three months later I stopped using the booklet and the trainer wheels came off. From that point a variety of reading systems have come my way which I have found helpful for accountability, staying on task and ensuring all 66 books are covered. Remember, if you read three to four chapters a day, you read the whole Bible in one year.

In this chapter I want to take you on the teaching journey that God has led me on during my ten-year walk with Him. It began with the Bible and has taken many pathways through some excellent resources. Putting this chapter together has shown me I've become a study junkie, but I hope it will encourage you to sit at the feet of Jesus and allow Him to teach you too. Before I write any more about this, let me first ask some questions.

How teachable are we? Think about when a child is open to being taught. There is no complaining, no rebelling, no sulking but an engaged individual who wants to learn. Are we like that with God? Consider someone you know who is – who has a situation arise in their life and sees God address it and they grow stronger through it. Do you struggle to be like that?

Much is taught in the book of Proverbs on life's most profound truths using simple, moral statements that highlight and teach fundamental realities about life.[1] Proverbs 1:7 says, 'The fear of the LORD is the beginning of knowledge; fools despise wisdom and instruction.' So for starters we must check the condition of our hearts. Are we teachable? Do we have a reverence for the Lord and come to His Word seeking to know Him? Or are we foolishly ignoring His wisdom and instruction in preference to addressing life issues with worldly philosophies and self-focused solutions.

Jesus taught out of the Scriptures. Luke 24:27 says, 'Then beginning with Moses and with all the prophets, He explained to them the things concerning Himself in all the Scriptures.' David refers to God's Word in Psalm 19 as 'the law of the Lord, the testimony of the Lord, the precepts of the Lord, the commandments, fear and judgments of the Lord.' He highlights the magnificence of God's Word as 'more desirable than gold, yes, than much fine gold; sweeter also than honey and the drippings of the honeycomb.' So we must read it! Not only is God's Word more desirable than gold but it should be:

- taught to children (Deuteronomy 6:7, 11:19; 2 Timothy 3:15)
- read (Deuteronomy 17:19; Isaiah 34:16)
- esteemed above all things (Job 23:12)
- meditated upon (Psalm 1:2; 119:99)
- longed for (Psalm 119:82)
- heard (Nehemiah 8:1)
- obeyed (Matthew 7:24; Luke 11:28; James 1:22)
- searched daily (Acts 17:11), and
- known (2 Timothy 3:15).[2]

This is only a partial list of commands and instructions, there are so many more.

As I have shared in previous chapters, God used His Word to draw me to Him and feed me. When I was baptised, family members bought me a MacArthur Study Bible. I have found it very useful to glean MacArthur's notes in order to more fully understand a passage of Scripture. I have heard it said that we should look at three to four different commentaries to understand more fully how to interpret Bible passages. There are some great free downloads online that can also assist, such as e-Sword and Bible Hub.

I want to share some information from the introductory pages of my Bible that have inspired me and I hope will inspire you to be passionate about God's Word. It starts with a portion of a quote from Martin Luther: 'Unless I am convicted by Scripture and plain reason – I do not accept the authority of popes and councils, for they have contradicted each other – my conscience is captive to the Word of God.' And MacArthur continues:

> This book contains: the mind of God, the state of man, the way of salvation, the doom of sinners, and the happiness of believers.
>
> Its doctrine is holy, its precepts are binding, its histories are true, and its decisions are immutable. Read it to be wise, believe it to be saved, and practice it to be holy.
>
> It contains light to direct you, food to support you, and comfort to cheer you. It is the traveller's map, the pilgrim's staff, the pilot's compass, the soldier's sword, and the Christian's charter. Here heaven is open, and the gates of hell are disclosed.
>
> Christ is the grand subject, our good its design, and the glory of God its end. It should fill the memory, rule the heart, and guide the feet.
>
> Read it slowly, frequently and prayerfully. It is a mine of wealth, health to the soul, and a river of pleasure. It is given to you here in this life, will be opened at the judgment, and is established forever.
>
> It involves the highest responsibility, will reward the greatest labour, and condemn all who trifle with its contents.[3]

Whenever I have women telling me they are struggling and not in a good place, I question them about their time in God's Word. Often they admit they have been neglecting their Bible reading. As a young Christian I found I would be vulnerable after three days if I failed to read the Word. Daily reading and studying to apply God's Word in our lives must be a habit we adhere to as religiously as we clean our teeth.

There are many sound authors who can assist us to understand the Word of God and its application in our life. The first to come my way was the *Self-confrontation Bible Study.*[4] In my opinion, this would have to be one of the most in-depth studies available. I did this the first time on my own and it gave me freedom from the devil's lies in a number of areas of my life. I felt chains of bondage break as I worked through its pages. It's still happening. As I repeat the study with others they also experience transformation. 'You learn how to face, deal with, and endure even the most difficult trials you may encounter in your personal relationships and circumstances.'[5] I have referred to this study book in previous chapters, citing the freedom it gave me in areas of responsibility. Another area in which I was challenged was contentment in singleness. Oddly enough this information is contained in the lessons on the marriage relationship. I was surprised how much attention was given to singleness in the two-part lessons on marriage. I gleaned a lot of helpful teaching. One paragraph in particular I would like to share:

> So if you are single, you should not be searching for a spouse. If the Lord has someone for you, nothing can keep you from meeting your future spouse. You never need to look. Instead, you are to focus on serving the Lord with all of your heart. In the process of serving the Lord, He may lead you to the one who is to be your husband or wife. But you are not to have that search be the

> focus of your life. You are to be content in the circumstances into which God has placed you, and delight in serving the Lord with all your energy.'[6]

We know that God is a God of order. Throughout the Bible He gives specific instructions for many situations. Studying a truth such as contentment in singleness meant another area of life came into order. When our lives are standing on God's truth there is more order and more freedom. 'For you were called to freedom, brethren; only *do* not *turn* your freedom into an opportunity for the flesh, but through love serve one another' (Galatians 5:13). It's quite simple really, isn't it! Love God, love others and watch God give your life order, simplicity and freedom. The next book I would like to share with you is *My Single Mom Life* by Angela Thomas.[7] God taught me a lot through this book as well as inspiring me to write. I had only been a Christian for three years when this book not only placed a calling on my life but showed me that my family of three, void of a dad in the home, was still very unique. Angela writes,

> I want you to understand and believe and desire that your life – yep, your single-mom life – can become a very amazing life. Our kids can rock the world, complete with tender hearts from emotional lessons learned early enough to give them a head start. You already know that being a single mom is the hardest job on the planet. We do more than anyone will probably ever appreciate or notice. The exhaustion that goes with this gig is nearly indescribable. But it can be done. A single mom with a houseful of kids can live a very beautiful life.'[8]

Ideally each family has a father and a mother who, as a team, raise their children. While I will always be sad for my children not growing up with a mum and dad in the home, I am really thankful they got to witness their mother's life being transformed by the grace of God. I learnt that my family of three is unique and very special to Him. At times I was vulnerable to the lies that 'broken families' are deficient and was anxious about the negative statistics for children of single parents. I learnt I wasn't alone in saying that single parents don't consider their family as unique. At a mental health training course I co-facilitated, a person described how her mother struggled with the status of the family following separation. She recalled when her dad left their family, her mother said to the children, on more than one occasion, that they were not a real family anymore! This is one of many lies I think we listen to in our vulnerability, tiredness and times of doubt that we have anything to offer. Angela Thomas' book is an easy read. It is full of fun, practical advice on raising healthy, happy children as a groovy single mom!

A different type of parental advice book that I also valued is *Shepherding a Child's Heart* by Tedd Tripp.[9] I was still a very young Christian when I first read this and I found it a bit heavy. I thought, *This book is for those solid, home-schooled families with both parents putting in consistent effort*. But a couple of years later I revisited it and found I liked the instruction and guidelines it provided and was able to implement some of the teaching. Through the grace of God I had grown and was able to absorb more of God's teaching and way of life than at first. Tripp's book is solid, biblically-based coaching on how to reach a child's heart through your words and actions. It also addresses the parent's heart and parent's discipline so be prepared to be assailed for all the right reasons!

The next study to come along was a Peacemaker Ministries resource called *The Young Peacemaker.*[10] This teaches children how to respond to conflict God's way and is a great resource, one you wish could be taught in schools. It is really practical and insightful on how to handle conflict whether in the home, workplace or school grounds.

There are twelve key principles for Young Peacemakers:

- Conflict is a slippery slope.
- Conflict starts in the heart.
- Choices have consequences.
- Wise-way choices are better than my-way choices.
- The blame game makes conflict worse.
- Conflict is an opportunity.
- The 5As can resolve conflict.
- Forgiveness is a choice.
- It's never too late to start doing what's right.
- Think before you speak.
- Respectful communication is more likely to be heard.
- A respectful appeal can prevent conflict.

> The immediate and long term goal of this study is for students to resolve conflict in a biblically faithful manner, to enjoy the freedom of restored relationships and develop godly character.[11]

I have not been so successful in finding solid books on teaching boys as I have for girls. Mostly my son got books like *The Pilgrim's Progress*[12] and *Keeping Holiday.*[13] One book addressing boys' character is *Checkpoints: A Tactical Guide to Manhood* by Mills and Wagnon,[14] but because it looks at pornography and addictions, the maturity level of your son needs to be taken into consideration. For my daughter I found Karen Andreola's book *Beautiful Girlhood*[15] a beneficial book for addressing good character. This book is written in old-school language but is practical and insightfully written for equipping girls. I also was gifted a pack entitled *Secret Keeper Girl: The Power of True Beauty and Modesty*[16] that really motivated me to have intimate, purposeful time with my daughter to remind her how special she is to me and to God.

For the first four years of my Christian walk I was completing social work studies so some fictional reading on my semester breaks was welcomed. Francine Rivers is a Christian author of mostly novels and I think she is one of the best! Francine Rivers has a gift of keeping faithful to Scripture while retelling biblical stories in her fictional writing. For example, *Redeeming Love* is based on the book of Hosea and set in the California gold rush days. I have come across a number of ladies who love to escape into a romance novel. Periodically reading authors like Francine Rivers is a safe way to get lost in this genre without the secular smut we should avoid. The range of about 30 books from this author includes both contemporary and historical fiction.

My first small group Bible study was a book called *Having a Mary Heart in a Martha World*[17] by Joanna Weaver. I repeated this study five years later and was quite captivated by her practical, humorous approach to learning. So I purchased her second and third books, *Having a Mary Spirit* and *Lazarus Awakening*. Recently I studied the second book in a small group, complete with a DVD so we could experience Joanna speaking to us in our living rooms! As the titles imply these studies focus on shaping our characters to be godly women, allowing God to change us from the inside out.

When my first child hit the teenage years I thank God for putting Paul Tripp's (yes, Tedd's brother) book *Age of Opportunity*[18] into my hands. This was one of those books that changed my life with its incredible timing and pivotal teaching. *Age of Opportunity* deals with parents' responses to events and situations in their teenagers' lives. As the title suggests, whatever your teen brings your way is an opportunity to align this with God's truths and promises. So when a serious situation arose about three months after reading this book, rather than a major freak-out and being totally overtaken by the situation, I thought, *Okay, so what needs to be taught and restored at this time?* This book addresses your teen's heart, equips them with wisdom and helps them think about their choices and actions.

A couple of studies I enjoyed doing with teenaged girls were *Lies Young Women Believe*[19] and *Girls Gone Wise in a World Gone Wild.*[20] The first one is also available as *Lies Women Believe and the Truth That Sets Them Free* so mother and daughter could do this together. Mary Kassian is the author of *Girls Gone Wise*. She has an interactional website with additional resources, including worksheets for each chapter. There is also a DVD addition to this study, using interviews from guys and giving advice to young ladies. One clip in particular gave sound advice on being a wife. This is a practical, insightful study and has a discussion topic early in the book which makes it suitable for older girls. One woman I know organised a group of girls and had a fun, bonding weekend doing a condensed version of the study. Follow that up with *Lies Young Women Believe* which also has a workbook. This study doesn't hold back and really tackles the heart of problems and the deception of the devil. Again, this is a practical, insightful study that would also be suitable for older girls due to the descriptive types of stories it contains.

Elizabeth George has a number of great books addressing life management and the pursuit of godliness for women. Also available from this author are studies for girls as young as possibly eight years; for example, *A Girl's Guide to Making Really Good Choices*[21] and for the college-aged girls, *A Young Woman's Guide to Making Good Choices*. I recommend these for one-on-one mother-and-daughter time as they are easy, practical studies.

About four years ago I came across Jerry Bridges' book *Respectable Sins.*[22] I appreciated the challenge as God addressed the subtle sins in my life. I hadn't considered discontentment to be a sin until I read this book, so this got some necessary attention! I was excited when a couple of years later a study book was produced. Studying this in a small group engendered much discussion and, this time, impatience really stood out to me! Bridges is another reliable author and has written many great books including *Trusting God* and *The Pursuit of Holiness*.

John MacArthur produces some wonderful study group material. You would be hard pressed to find a biblical topic that MacArthur has not written about. If your group wanted to do a book of the Bible this is a good place to go. One study I have been chipping away at is *Experiencing the Passion of Christ*. This study focuses closely on Christ's movements prior to arrest and finishes with the aftermath of the crucifixion and the resurrection. I love the attention to detail, learning such things as, for example:

> Gethsemane was a garden planted with olive trees ... On that site today there is still a thriving olive grove, with a few trees more than two thousand years old. Those very trees may well have been mute witnesses to the drama on that fateful evening.[23]

If there is an aspect or event in the Bible that intrigues you and you want to study it more closely, MacArthur is one writer who will give a sound perspective.

Over a year ago I started a biblical counselling course that initially covered theology and then gave lectures on specific counselling topics such as medical issues and counselling problems. The material came out of the United States and utilises a lot of Jay E. Adams' material. Adams is a pioneer in biblical counselling and has written many books which demonstrate his strong belief in the Bible's sufficiency to address any problem in a Christian's life. Two of his books are entitled *Christian Living in the Home*[24] and *Marriage, Divorce and Remarriage in the Bible*.[25] The first gives a practical, somewhat older-fashioned approach to the home and family, while the latter is a must-read for a biblical perspective on legitimate divorce and remarriage. If you are interested in deepening your knowledge of every believer's call to counsel others, then Adams' material will enhance that call. Books such as *Competent to Counsel* and *How to Help People Change* are a good starting point.

Recently I have been drawn into deeper studies through a training programme and introduced to Wayne Grudem's book on *Bible Doctrine*.[26] What an amazing book to learn more about the Christian faith; it has in-depth looks at such topics as the attributes of God and the Trinity. This book highlights the levels of learning that God will take you to.

So while this has been a small glimpse of one believer's walk with a handful of resources, I hope it has encouraged you in your walk. God has blessed us with many great Christian authors, old and new. I haven't even mentioned Charles Spurgeon in this chapter, yet his Bible commentaries have inspired me to 'soar into the loftiest regions of spiritual thought.'[27] Other great authors of our past include C.S. Lewis and John Newton, and there are libraries full of many, many great writing saints of old. These are just a tiny handful and I'm sure you will have much more to add.

Finally, we must beware of material that teaches false doctrine. We must be mindful of psychology added as a *prescription,* when its only place in our teaching is as a *description* of human development and learning. I use the guideline that if God appears as a tokenism, I will avoid the material. We must seek to devour only those books which use Scripture clearly and precisely. We must follow the example of the Bereans when they first encountered Paul's preaching: 'With great eagerness ... [they examined] the Scriptures daily to see whether these things were so' (Acts 17:11).

Chapter 7

He Supports Me

I would like to share briefly an experience of a single mum very dear to me. Unlike me, she was raised in a Christian family and has always known a church family. She was devastated when her marriage ended. This was not the plan! Initially it would have been easy to stop attending church as she battled with the emotions and shock of her situation but she made herself go for the sake of her children. There was never any intention to turn away from church as God was always first priority. Four years later she approached me when I was new to her church. We became instant friends. We started doing the self-confrontation study, blending our two families every Friday night, beginning with a meal. This study lasted for about two years and she found it helped switch her view from self to God.

My friend's frequent statement is 'God provides'. On several occasions she would go to the mailbox and there would be an envelope of money, just the right amount needed. To this day she still doesn't know who did this, but is so thankful to God for His provision. God has provided her with much on her journey including support from family, support from church outreaches such as the op shop, and through serving on the money course run by Christians Against Poverty (CAP).[1] Her life group maintains regular study and the play group connects her with other mums. Among all of this there have been random acts of kindness that help her to see she is loved and not alone. I must add that she is always the first to encourage others with a meal or baking, a card at a time of need, a listening ear and serving at church. Many women have been blessed by my friend.

Encouragement for the single mum is important, as it is for all mothers. Encouragement is tied in very closely with support and when you ask people to share about how they have been supported, some will share with thankfulness while others relay a story full of rejection and bitterness. In this chapter we will first look at how we can encourage others and support them as well as looking at how God encourages us. Lastly, I address how we can reach out to others.

As we consider our individual responsibility to encourage others, let's look at some verses showing the importance of being connected to a body of believers.

> Let us hold fast the confession of our hope without wavering, for He who promised is faithful; and let us consider how to stimulate one another to love and good deeds, not forsaking our own assembling together, as is the habit of some, but encouraging one another; and all the more as you see the day drawing near. (Hebrews 10:23-25)

And these encouraging verses:

> Shout joyfully to the LORD, all the earth.
> Serve the LORD with gladness;

Come before Him with joyful singing.
Know that the LORD Himself is God;
It is He who has made us, and not we ourselves;
We are His people and the sheep of His pasture.
(Psalm 100:1-3)

The church matters to Christ. It is His body of believers that is to witness to a lost world (Acts 1:8) and that is to one day be complete in Him (Colossians 1:28). Do you regularly attend a church? Do you view church as supportive and loving or judgmental and distant? Are you going to church for the reasons described in the verses above – to stimulate and encourage one another? What if we were simply thankful to have a building where we can come together to worship, regardless of how amazing we sound or who is doing what? What if our focus was on His two commands: loving Him and loving others? Focusing on Him rather than the sideways look we thought someone gave us. What say we tuned out to self-focused thoughts and tuned in to the words of the songs that praise and worship God? Often those words tell of His love for us. They also tell of what Jesus has done for us and of His power.

The predominant teaching theme that runs through this book is 'Read the Bible!' It is pivotal in our growth as Christians. We should be stimulating and encouraging one another. So in order to look at this topic of encouragement, I suggest we first look at ourselves (Matthew 7:3). How are we walking with the Lord? Do we have expectations that others should carry us, feed us and stimulate us? Support and encouragement is a two-way relationship so take a moment to prayerfully evaluate yourself:

Do I grumble about people in my church?

1 2 3 4 5 6 7 8 9 10
(Never) (All the time)

Do I come to church with an expectation of others meeting my needs?

1 2 3 4 5 6 7 8 9 10
(Never) (All the time)

Do I encourage others or expect them to encourage me?

1 2 3 4 5 6 7 8 9 10
(Encourage others) (Expect encouragement)

If you score more than 15 in these three questions, then you may need to take time to prayerfully ask God why.

Always, when we need support we should bow before God in prayer. It occurred to me one day that when struggles came along, the first thing I did was pick up the phone and call my sister. This is all good and fine but, as a believer, the first place I should go is to God in prayer and to His Word (see Chapter 9 for more about praying). He never fails. He is always there. Never too busy. Always waiting to hear. Always has plenty of time for me. And His Word is full of encouragement.

Now we have addressed our individual responsibility, let's look at some verses in the Bible on encouragement for single mums. In the book of Titus there are some areas that are mentioned that younger women can be encouraged in:

> Encourage the young women to ... love their children, to be sensible, pure, workers at home, and kind ... so that the word of God will not be dishonoured. (Titus 2:4-5)

So let us look at each of these areas:

Loving our children

'Children are a gift from the LORD, they are a reward from Him' (Psalm 127:3, NLT). I remember hearing a sermon about children being a gift and thinking, *Oh my, sometimes in the drudgery of day-to-day life I forget this!* Martha Peace writes:

> A mother is to think of her child as beloved or dear [however] all mothers struggle to one degree or another with impatience. Some are even mean and hard-hearted. Some selfishly neglect their children. Regardless of how little or how much they love their children, all mothers could benefit from occasional help and encouragement.[2]

A practical way to assist with thinking loving thoughts is to have the love verses from 1 Corinthians 13:4-7 attached to your mirror or fridge door.

> Love is patient, love is kind and is not jealous; love does not brag and is not arrogant, does not act unbecomingly; it does not seek its own, is not provoked, does not take into account a wrong suffered, does not rejoice in unrighteousness, but rejoices with the truth; bears all things, believes all things, hopes all things, endures all things.

Being sensible

Other Bible translations use the words self-controlled, sober-minded and discreet.

One commentator says this means 'to bear a good personal character, not vain and rash.'[3] I am really thankful to have learnt to prioritise my role as a parent and battle against selfishness. I worked and studied but my children took priority. Time invested in them was more important than getting my degree or working a full-time position. We need to stay alert to the choices we make; to be self-controlled and wise in order to protect our relationship with our children. This will also protect energy levels. There is plenty to fill each day. Wise choices to manage time – ensuring the need to rest and spend time with God – will help mums to avoid being overwhelmed.

In Chapter 5 I discussed being sensible with money: staying within budget and paying bills. This is an area that can easily overwhelm us. Just look at the New Zealand Census on how most are faring:

In 2013, the percentage of families receiving a family income (from all sources) of $40,000 or less was 60.6 percent for one-parent families.

The median family income from all sources varied according to family type, for example:

- couples without children had a median family income of $70,900
- one-parent families had a median family income of $33,100
- couples with child(ren) had a median family income of $92,000.[4]

God will always provide. I have seen that often first-hand, and I want to really encourage you about that. However, sometimes a change of heart is needed on how we view our financial situation. While we see the median income for single parent families is low, there are ways we can seek support through each week. Currently my church is running CAP courses which look closely at budgeting and money management. Perhaps look for one in your region or seek someone from within your church or community who is an accountant or finance person. Often another person's perspective can help us see areas we may have overlooked.

Lastly, I want to encourage sensible thinking. We need to guard our thoughts so that we don't lose valuable time thinking the worst. It's been said that 'worry is like a rocking chair – it gives you something to do, but it doesn't get you anywhere.' One interesting set of statistics indicates that there is nothing we can do about 70 percent of our worries. Of the things we worry about:

- 40% will never happen.
- 30% are about the past – which can't be changed.
- 12% are about criticism from others, mostly untrue.
- 10% are about health, which gets worse with stress.
- 8% are about real problems that can be solved.[5]

So be sure to dwell on what is true, right, pure, lovely and admirable – 'if anything is excellent and praiseworthy – think about such things' (Philippians 4:8, NIV).

Being pure

I consider this a really important area that often gets overlooked. A single mum needs protection and support against carnality and self-pleasing.

Very rarely do we discuss sexual sin openly. The Bible has many verses, such as Matthew 15:18-20, about how innately we have wrong thoughts, and about sexual sin which defiles us. Single mums are no exception and can be easily tempted to sinfully daydream, have sexual fantasies and seek self-gratification. The media draws us into thinking Mr Right will ride in on his big steed like a knight in shining armour. The temptation to immoral thoughts and actions is one that must be addressed decisively: 'Take every thought captive to the obedience of Christ' (2 Corinthians 10:5). This is a vital response and there are several ways to implement it, such as repeating Scripture, singing a hymn or worship song, or by praying. Left unaddressed, guilt and shame can do real damage. Accountability is another effective way to address this decisively. Let someone know you are struggling so they can encourage you to stand strong.

The desire to be cherished and loved by a man can lead one into unhealthy relationships. The consequences of an unhealthy relationship and what it may ultimately cost, may cause a lot of turmoil. Words of encouragement and teaching about God's mercy to people who repent can restore a woman to freedom and joy in Christ. Remember that God designed the joy and intimacy of a sexual relationship to be experienced only between a husband and wife (Hebrews 13:4). This means trusting God regardless of the plan He has for our lives. In the meantime, single mums must be encouraged to see that walking with God, honouring and obeying Him, can give a full, satisfying life. I can personally attest to this. Although I had many struggles and am far from having a perfect record, God protected me and kept me desiring Him above all else.

Working at home

A woman's home should be one of her top priorities. There are four proverbs that speak to this:

- Wisdom has built her house (Proverbs 9:1)
- The wise woman builds her house (Proverbs 14:1)
- By wisdom a house is built, and by understanding it is established; and by knowledge the rooms are filled with all precious and pleasant riches (Proverbs 24:3-4)
- She looks well to the ways of her household (Proverbs 31:27)[6]

To have a well-managed, organised home is such a blessing for all who occupy and visit it. While I have never been a diligent cleaner of the home I do strive to keep it organised. While some women act like a slave to their home and never seem content with its appearance, I believe there is a fine balance. And I believe the key to this is routine.

Once I finally learnt to live by a consistent routine, I found more was being achieved. I have two set days for writing and reading, I walk most mornings, have study groups on two days and do housework on one day. You may be gasping right now at the thought of only one day for housework. While I do need to be more diligent in this department, my point is that once you work out what is the best routine for your week, the key is then to *stick at it!*

My sister would talk to me about her meal plan and I would scoff at the idea, saying I preferred to be spontaneous. When it became apparent that I needed more structure in my life, I also implemented a meal plan. Wow, what a difference! I began doing one big shop a week as opposed to four or six dashes to the supermarket. A master list reminds me of meals I can cook, with a set Thursday night roast, a chilled Friday homemade takeaway-style meal, a light dish on Sunday night and a quick easy Wednesday night meal since that's a crazy night in our home. What I have enjoyed most about this meal plan is it has taken away having to think on a daily basis about what to cook, which, most of us would agree, is the hardest part.

As I mentioned in Chapter 5 and earlier in this chapter, I urge you to be careful about time spent outside of the home. Even when children are in their teen years, the presence of Mum in the home is still very important. Do fight hard for having family-friendly work hours. I have one single-mum friend who does in-home childcare so she can work from home. There may be some sacrifices but home life must take priority over earning money: 'Make sure that your character is free from the love of money, being content with what you have' (Hebrews 13:5). Delighting in your home, whether you own it or not, begins with your state of mind. Contentment, gratitude and love for the Lord will help you see that even if you are skint in terms of earthly possessions, you are abundantly rich as a child of God.

Being kind

I want to reiterate here how important it is to be at peace with people because bitterness and anger can rob us of the ability to be kind.

When children have just one parent in the home, there is a greater sense of responsibility to have a right relationship with them – they don't have the other parent to run to for comfort if we are being unfair or unkind. There should always be someone they can ring such as a grandparent, aunty or significant person if they need a listening ear. If any reader cannot think who this person could be, then you face the task of investing time into relationships for your children's sake. You may have unconsciously isolated yourself from relationships and, in so doing, you have isolated your children from necessary care and support. Please prayerfully consider taking a step towards having significant people in your family's lives to enrich the work you are doing.

It is easy to get into a rut of seeing the things our children do wrong. Therefore, it is important for us to appeal to God for patience and wisdom rather than critically addressing every fault. Proverbs 19:11 says, 'A man's discretion makes him slow to anger, and it is his glory to overlook a transgression.' This Proverb does not imply we overlook sin – it says *a* transgression, singular. And Jesus often said 'go and sin no more.' It is when we notice a pattern of sin in our children's lives, that we need to address it. Refer back to Chapter 5 on advice about discipline and instruction which suggests focusing on one or two concerns at a time.

I found when I wasn't walking around with my 'sin-radar', I was more likely to be gracious. Our words and actions should be expressing love and kindness to our children. Proverbs 31:26 says, 'She opens her mouth in wisdom, and the teaching of kindness is on her tongue.' This is what we want to aspire to. I would like to etch that verse into my glasses so I can be reminded of it every moment!

When our behaviour is godly, we are also instilling into our children how to be adults. This is especially true for our daughters when we are joyfully role-modelling running a home and raising them. Recently my daughter celebrated the end of her schooling and is now in her first year at university. I am amazed at how fast the time has gone. I often used to think we were in a time-warp and my children would be young for years and years. I had not considered that one day I would be facing the last years of having them under my roof. I ask myself, *Am I teaching her all she needs to know while she is under my protection?* This teaching includes finances, relationships, work ethics and most importantly, having God at the centre of it all. Just as God supports us, teaching us in the ways we should go (Psalm 32:8), so we must support our children in a steadfast, loving, gentle way.

So these are five points to be encouraged in. The verses which teach them also say that it is older women who can do this teaching. Because my oldest child was five when Mum died, I really missed having her encouragement and wisdom in my life. When I became a Christian and discovered these verses, I approached an older woman. We purposed to meet regularly and did a study together. She became like a mother to me.

I had a young mother say she would like an older woman in her life but she struggled to instigate it. She also finds reaching out and talking to others hard. I suggested that she first consider what may be causing her difficulty. For example, shyness may be a self-focus problem or worrying about what other people think may be a man-pleasing problem. There are potentially many reasons why someone may struggle, so prayerfully ask God for help. Consider talking with someone who knows you really well. You want to discover the heart of the problem, not just look at your behaviour but what is underlying that behaviour.

List any sinful thoughts or actions – there may be things you need to change. And, if need be, you may have to seek forgiveness for these. In order to make any changes you have identified as necessary, meditate on God's word for what you need to 'put off' (stop doing) and what you need to 'put on' (start doing). For example, if you find that you struggle talking with others because you often end up gossiping then look at this verse: 'But have nothing to do with worldly fables fit only for old women. On the other hand, discipline yourself for the purpose of godliness' (1 Timothy 4:7). Here is a clear command to 'put off' talking in terms of worldly philosophies and gossiping, and discipline yourself to be a godly woman. We must make sure not to just look at what we need to put off (change). We must replace it with a right way of living. Once you have worked on your list of put-offs and put-ons you should then work on a specific plan to start talking with others. Here is another example:

- stay behind after the church service to have a cup of coffee
- then, ask someone how their week has been
- stay after the service for coffee for a month and connect with someone friendly
- then, ask that person to your house or a café for a cuppa.

All the while you are implementing your plan, humbly seek God's direction and pray a lot. You are seeking God to change *you* – do not think that if you struggle to find a friendly connection the fault lies with others and *they* have to change. While this may be the case, it is God's domain to change others.

Also, be sure to have a plan for your children, especially for little ones who are too heavy to hold for long periods. Small children need to learn to share their mother. As you plan, prepare your child to understand you are going to stay behind for a short while and would like them to wait quietly beside you. Be very sure to keep it a short while; do not exasperate them with a lengthy wait. If they follow this instruction, consider something like stopping at the dairy on the way home and rewarding them with a dollar mixture of lollies to say thank you. I'm not a fan of offering rewards with instructions but rather surprising them with a reward later. The reason being, children are wired to whinge, haggle and manipulate to get the reward whether they have followed the instruction or not. *They* are focused on the reward, *you* want them to learn to follow instructions. The following week you may find they will want to dictate the getting of more lollies. This is again an opportunity to remind them to follow instructions and see what happens. If they fail to obey – such as starting to grumble or expecting a reward – then slip in a disappointment.

If you have a child that struggles with not getting their own way perhaps wait to tell them the bad news once you are driving out of the parking lot. Cope with their temper tantrum till you get home and then discipline once you are home. In this process you are giving the instructions, setting the guidelines and expectations.

If you remain consistent and do not exasperate or ignore your child, over time you will train them to the point you can stay behind for fellowship after the service. Having colouring books, others to play with or a book to read will also help. This is such an important area in which to train your children. Don't give up.

If you look but struggle to find an older woman, don't lose heart. Keep praying and trust God will provide what you need when you need it. In her book, Martha Peace considers reasons why older women struggle to disciple younger women. She writes:

> The matter is likely due to wrong thinking and responses on the part of the older woman and the younger woman. The older woman may be afraid that something unpleasant might transpire. She probably grew up with the belief that you do not say anything unless the other person asks for help. On the other hand, the younger woman may be proud and become defensive if anyone thinks she is less than perfect. She probably grew up with the belief that if anyone reproves her they are not accepting her as she is, not loving her, and making her feel badly ... The process should be as natural as slipping your hand into a glove that fits perfectly. If both will do what is right – the older one reaching out in love to the younger and the younger one responding in humility with a teachable heart – God will be glorified, the older woman will overcome her fear, and the younger woman will grow in grace by leaps and bounds.[7]

Here is a list of encouraging characteristics and activities that supported me in my single-mum walk:

Being loved – While only God can change me, I appreciated being encouraged in love to grow and be the best I could be.

Having hope – Some days I struggled but knowing someone was there to encourage me, helped turn hopelessness into hopefulness.

Being responsible – I was encouraged to take a realistic approach to tasks and keep focused on my responsibilities.

Being honest – I learnt to value open, honest communication but not to the extent of exhausting anyone or having them think they were taken for granted.

Being educated – I appreciated encouraging, biblical books; wise insights; and going to seminars or women's events.

Receiving support – Sometimes this was a listening ear, help in the garden, with babysitting or going out for coffee so I could feel like an adult.

Remember that all people are sinners and sin; we all mess up from time to time. Quality support can be lacking. Assumptions can be made and so can mistakes. Remember that no one can read minds. If someone has done something to offend you, they genuinely may not realise and may not have intended to offend. It is so important to learn to communicate. If you struggle with being vulnerable with people, consider the following verses:

> In God I have put my trust, I shall not be afraid. What can man do to me? (Psalm 56:11)

> It is better to take refuge in the LORD than to trust in man. (Psalm 118:8)

> We had the sentence of death within ourselves so that we would not trust in ourselves, but in God who raises the dead. (2 Corinthians 1:9)

'Love the Lord your God with all your heart, and with all your soul, and with all your mind, and with all your strength.' The second [commandment] is this, 'You shall love your neighbour as yourself.' There is no other commandment greater than these. (Mark 12:30-31)

Chapter 8

A Daughter's Story

by Jessie

Jessie writes: Telling my story has never come easy to me. I've always looked upon it as my own personal secret, something I hold very close. That is until Mum proposed the idea that my story could actually help someone and asked if I would write a chapter. At first I thought, *What would someone possibly gain from hearing about my life?* But, as I started to think over my life and what has happened, what I have learnt and how my family and I have grown, I realised I have something I could share. So, I have written my life story for you hoping and praying that it provides insight and understanding into a child's journey through divorce.

Normality

By now you will have heard a lot of my story from Mum's previous chapters, but now you can hear it from me. Growing up, I never knew a family to be a mum, a dad and children. I had grown up with two separated parents and it never really registered that my family was any different to anybody else's. It was what it was. Mum and Dad had separated and Dad had moved away. I believe I saw it that way because my parents were civil – they normalised our situation. It reminds me of the saying:

'Don't let the children know Mummy and Daddy are fighting.' What went on behind the scenes of the divorce, what caused it and when it happened, stayed far away from the ears of my little brother and myself. I thank both my parents for their shelter at that time as I was able to live out a normal childhood. What I mean by 'normal' is that I was never disadvantaged by having a single parent; there simply never seemed to be anything different. At the dinner table it was always us three. At sports games, it was always just Mum on the sideline and it was always Mum organising and planning the birthday parties. But, although Dad lived quite some distance from us, he was occasionally at these events as well and their support was mutual. What I'm trying to portray here is that having a single parent should never feel like anything but a family. Because it is a family.

Mum, my brother and I, were a family. Mum never treated it like a burden or acted as if it was painful to raise us on her own. Of course, now that I am older, I understand that it would have undoubtedly been hard but she never showed it. My conclusion to that? The separation wasn't our fault. No separation is the fault of a child; the fault lies with the parents. This might sound harsh, but it's true. Unfortunately, marriages don't always work out and sometimes marriage partners split. My life continued to be normal because my parents understood the situation and knew their kids were not to blame. I never felt different and I never thought our family was different because of the situation in which Mum raised us.

Contentment

There was a great contentment in Mum and I think it reflected on me and my brother. Of course, we could always have had more – more money, more help and so on. For Mum, she had it all: us kids, a home, enough money and, as the years went on, she had a merciful God. It was Mum's acceptance of this situation and her determination to give her children the best lives possible that caused our contentment. Her contentment showed in never seeing any other men; there were no one-night stands, no boyfriends hanging around. She was content with being a single mum. Contentment is very peaceful for children – almost a reassuring promise that everything is okay. With this said, I cannot talk about the contentment Mum and my family had without talking about where it came from.

During Mum's single parenthood, as you would have already read, she found the Lord. It's actually quite remarkable how clear the difference is between an unbelieving mother and a believing one. A peace and a grace can be seen in the believing mother. Our mum's persona changed and that's where the contentment could be seen. In the hard times or trials that our family faced, Mum knew we would be taken care of. Even though she didn't see it at the time, she rested in the assurance that God would prevail. After Mum became a Christian, God became the centre of our family. All of her teaching and discipline was either from the Bible or from biblical books. God became the foundation of our family and it gave us all a sense of purpose. We didn't just live for ourselves any more. How we operated as a family wasn't for ourselves, it was for God. We lived for God. People often use the term 'life-changing' and I often thought that was a feel-good, over-the-top expression. But Mum becoming a Christian was truly life-changing and lifesaving. God saved Mum's life.

It wasn't long before my brother and I became Christians too. Mum had been taking us to a kids' camp in Rotorua for years which is where Jack and I gave our hearts to the Lord. After that, life was not spontaneously fantastic. It was still hard in that we continued to have our struggles and trials. However, Mum taught us constantly that God had engraved us on the palms of His hands (Isaiah 49:16) and that God was always with us, watching and guiding us.

Hardship

Although Mum protected and sheltered us from 'the situation', there was always a sense of wanting to know what happened and why it happened. For me this came when I started college. We had just moved from our small country town of Marton, to Upper Hutt in order to be closer to my dad. The move was fine and, to be honest, I was glad to be out of the small town and into a bigger city. We started going to a great church where I knew some people from a previous camp and I was able to kick off some friendships pretty easily. The college I attended wasn't our original choice, but my dad wanted me to go to a girls-only private school. This turned out to be a wonderful choice. So for the first couple of months everything was great with the move. We had a nice little home, I was closer to my dad, I was establishing great school friends, enjoying church; I was happy. As I write this I wish I could stop at this point and just pretend this is how it stayed. Unfortunately, it took a turn for the worse.

As my friendships developed I began to go around to my friends' houses to hang out and have dinner with them and their families. At first it was nice and secretly I once pretended it was my family with a mum and a dad and siblings. But as it went on and I continually saw 'happy' families with mums and dads together, I began to ask questions and become increasingly unhappy.

As a teenager I now questioned the sheltering I had been thankful for as a child. Questioning is not a bad thing. I think it is healthy if children ask questions and want to know why their parents separated and, regardless of their age, there should be discussions about it. Unfortunately my questions were not healthy: Was it my fault? What did I do wrong? Could I have stopped them? Why did Dad leave? Wasn't I good enough? These questions are ugly questions and far from the truth, but at the time they were what I was asking. From this time on, I entered into a spiral. I became increasingly unhappy and ended up absolutely hating myself. I am not one to talk about my feelings. I am a very 'closed-book' kind of person and so, as a 14-year-old, I believed my only resort was to keep it inside; this resulted in self-harming. I did it continuously at home and at school. I wanted to hurt and to feel pain because I despised myself for breaking up my parents' marriage. I was slowly slipping away from reality and, to tell you the truth, half of my Year 9 is a blank because I was just so detached.

My dad and his partner, who had three children from a previous marriage, were becoming quite serious, after having been together for a few years. Unfortunately, in my depressed state, I saw this as a replacement – he had found a better family. To watch your dad create a life with a family and partner you have never really fitted in with is hard. As time went on, my depression got worse and I turned to suicide as a solution. Twice I attempted it. Without going into too much detail, I want to explain I felt like there was nothing left. I was completely empty. I had turned away from God at this point but still attended church so I wouldn't draw attention to myself or have Mum suspect anything. But in true motherly fashion she had already suspected and before school one day she confronted me.

The next few months consisted of counselling sessions. For the first few I hardly spoke and flat out didn't want to be there. I was shut off and felt that no one was going to get me to open up. This changed one day when I saw the amount Mum was paying for the counselling and guilt set in. At first it wasn't easy to talk. It was extremely painful, but I am thankful that I did. Over more sessions, the counsellor helped me to understand what I was going through and why. It was quite remarkable. Through biblical verses and guidance, we tracked through my life which helped me understand not only the current situation but also me as a person. It wasn't an instant fix and a year later, when my mother met someone, I turned to drinking.

I went to parties to get drunk and used alcohol at night to help me sleep. Once more I was wrestling with this hatred of myself because, this time, Mum had replaced me. I wanted to feel numb, no pain and no hurt. It lasted a couple of months until my best friend found out and worked me through it. We wrestled through previous issues again and with what was happening. I came to the realisation that the situation wasn't as I saw it. It wasn't easy, I had a lot of bitterness towards Dad and his family, Mum and her new family, and myself for not fitting into any of it.

As the years have gone by it is still hard and has taken a while to heal. I have grown very close to the Lord, who has strengthened me and I have rested in Him for help. I look back at my depression and the trials I went through as a real reminder that I didn't understand why my parents had split and I had never asked. Although it was an extremely hard couple of years, to be honest, it taught me a lot. I have more understanding and awareness that what I used to think and believe was far from the truth. As I write this I need to make clear one thing. These feelings don't just go away. I still battle anger about the divorce, displacement by new families and sadness that my parents aren't together. These feelings are not wrong but the way they are dealt with is important. My mistake was that I never talked. So I urge you to talk about what you have experienced, to understand what happened and to work through the issues or questions that you have.

Reflection

I have tried to write this chapter about five times. Each version was very different from the last. Every time I rewrote the chapter I saw it from a different angle. Some versions were filled with anger, others with sadness, but most of them with a sense of happiness. I look at working through these versions not as a bad thing, but one that shows the emotion and journey I have been on as the daughter of a single mum.

Divorce is hard not only for the parents but for children. As a child you see a family you once had split apart and you want that family again. There are many emotions that are normal to feel. But sometimes in life things happen that are out of our control. In my story, my parents divorced and this affected my whole life. It's easy to think that everything is going to be so different or going to be weird with only one parent. It is easy to think about how it affects your life and sometimes it's easy to look at it negatively. It's easy to hate the separation and see that nothing good can come from a divorce. But sometimes, taking a step back, you can often see a positive side by looking at the good that has come or the memories that have been shared.

It is good that Mum has someone in her life. This is obviously easier said than done and it has taken me ten years to be able to do this, but looking at a divorce from a different angle can change your whole perspective.

As I look back on my life and the journey that I have had, I have one piece of advice, something I would have done differently. That is to *talk*. Talk to your parents about what happened, hear it from them and hopefully gain understanding. Talk to your siblings if you have them and lean on each other through it. Talk to others who have been through the same thing and talk to God because He always listens. Children are not alone in a divorce and they should never feel that way.

What Mum has taught me through her being a single mother is that we are not different and we are a family, regardless of how many parents sit at the dinner table. My mother raised me and my brother with security, love and wisdom and she did a damn good job alone! It was not easy and at times it still isn't, but together and by being there for each other, we get through.

Jessie marrying her best friend.

Chapter 9

He Answers Prayer

In 2006 when I became a Christian I learnt that all decisions need to be covered with much prayer. When I look back over my prayer life there have been some consistent periods. One in particular was prayer for my children as the teen years drew closer. I needed to pray for support in parenting teenagers. I prayed at length for guidance on where to live when my oldest child was ready for college, knowing that the small town where we lived was not where we wanted to stay. I believed the latter was answered when I decided to relocate back to the Wellington region. This took us closer to my sister, my children's dad and his parents.

I recall a day when my oldest was unwell and I had an important meeting at work that would not have been wise to cancel. I rang their nana to see if she could babysit and she was quick to say 'yes'. As I dropped Jessie to her I reflected upon my prayers for support and thanked God for answering them. Little did I know that soon He would orchestrate an even greater level of support.

By God's grace the three of us have been called into His family. In 2016 Jessie made a public declaration in baptism to say she would follow Christ. While we don't dwell on it, we know if it weren't for God we would be in such a different state. After Jessie's difficult first year of college, I witnessed God build her up. Year after year she became stronger and more determined. Throughout the preceding years she had experienced some physical health issues and one of these brought me to the realisation that my children belong firstly to God. This strengthened me and enabled me to step back and let God speak into her life. I needed to pray, and I did. Prayer was answered in a variety of ways including her church mates texting verses regularly and her putting, 'I am fearfully and wonderfully made' from Psalm 139, prominently on her wall. And through prayer God was settling me. God kept me stable and focused on Him so He could have me be what He needed me to be for Jessie. Don't miss this very simple, important point – stay focused on Christ.

Exactly one year after Jessie's baptism, Jack was baptised as well. Here is the testimony he shared with our church:

> Hey, I'm Jack, for all who don't know me. I was raised by my mum, Jo, to understand God's Word and I have always believed that God exists. I never thought there was a possibility of any other alternative, and I went to church every Sunday.
>
> Up until recently I felt as though I wasn't all that bad and had the mentality, *Well I sin much less than the rest of my worldly friends, so I guess I'm alright.* But now God has shown me that I truly am a sinner in need of a saviour, and He has led me to the realisation that I didn't really understand what it meant to be a Christian.
>
> I have learnt that I can't handle the sin in my life by myself and that I must lay it before God. I realised that my faith has always been temperamental – I would turn

up to church and youth group thinking, *I am a Christian* but as soon as I left the building I would live for myself and become worldly again. All my time and the things on my mind were full of the things of this world. God was only getting a small portion of me on Sundays and Wednesdays (youth group). My life was filled with self-centredness and all my time would go into the things I wanted, not what God wanted for me.

A verse that has helped me tremendously is Matthew 6:24 (NIV), 'No one can serve two masters; for either he will hate the one and love the other, or he will be devoted to one and despise the other. You cannot serve God and wealth.' This verse has worked wonders in my life as God has led me to realise I cannot serve this world and my own pleasures. I need to fully devote my life to Him and always have Him in the forefront of my mind.

I have learnt that knowing the Word is not enough, that I need to apply it each day to every aspect of my life. God has taught me to lay all the things of this world aside and have Him at the centre.

I want to leave you with one of my favourite verses, Matthew 16:24, 'Then Jesus said to his disciples, "If anyone wants to come after me, he must deny himself, and take up his cross and follow me."'

God is the only true master and I am thankful He led me to become a Christian.

Thank you.

Recently the movie *War Room* inspired me to want to be a better prayer warrior. Occasions like taking the dog for a morning walk, can be a good opportunity to pray specifically for family members. You may be able to relate to a problem that can creep in to prayer life: the difficulty of keeping one's mind on the task of praying. For example, I'm walking along with my dog praying when I see a nice garden. Then, before I know it I'm thinking about what's for tea and whether I bought cheese in the last groceries. I'm fascinated at the weird tangents my mind can go. My pastor's wife gave me a great suggestion: allocate a portion of the walk to specific people. We came up with a plan right there and then. I would start with prayer for family as I headed off down the hill, my oldest along the stretch, my son for up the hill and round the corner, and so forth. When I put it into action it worked well and there was even time left over to pray for the church elders and other pressing situations.

As I worked on this chapter, I continued to come back to a common theme: We are to be faithful and God takes care of the results. I first mentioned and unpacked this briefly in Chapter 4. This one line of twelve words could easily become a book. Consider the following verses:

> Be anxious for nothing, but in everything by prayer and supplication with thanksgiving let your requests be made known to God. And the peace of God, which surpasses all comprehension, will guard your hearts and your minds in Christ Jesus. (Philippians 4:6-7)

This is just one example out of thousands in the Bible demonstrating that in our role as servants of Christ, we are to be anxious for nothing, giving prayer with thanksgiving. It is God who guards our hearts in Christ Jesus. Praying is a fundamental aspect of the Christian life. For a number of years, I would say that I was 'dutiful' in my prayers, copying how others prayed and believing that God was hearing. Scripture says that He hears the prayers of the righteous (Psalm 34:15; Proverbs 15:29; John 9:31), whereas remaining in a sinful state brings about separation and God will not hear us (Isaiah 59:2). Therefore I sought to repent of sins, asking the Lord to show me any wrongdoing where I may be offending Him. My prayer life was more ticking off a to-do list than heartfelt communing, although there were times of brokenness on bended knees crying out for help and mercy. Prayer is also essential to combat our drifting off into sinful thinking.

> God holds us responsible for how we think, speak, and act no matter how sinfully another person behaves.[1]

When I am mulling over hurtful words, personal irritations or the devil's attack in the wee hours of the morning, prayer or singing a worship song can soon cut through it. Sinful traps such as overthinking, grumbling and discontentment must be addressed quickly and decisively.

As I finish this book and look back over my story, I see how much God has changed me since I began to follow Christ. All He has orchestrated in my life. All His answers to prayer. How He takes care of all outcomes and has the final say. The results in every area of our lives: our finances, children, relationships, job, home, spiritual state of being. Everything. This ties in with prayer. We are to faithfully pray (and there is plenty of direction in His Word on how, when, what) and leave it with Him. In His right time and in His right way, He will answer. Give all to God and you will have all you need.

Chapter 10

Final Reflections

Throughout my journey as a single mum, I occasionally wrestled with God about the struggles of doing life as a single parent. I have shared that initially my 'temper tantrums' were lengthy and extreme. I questioned God as to how long I would be on my own. I watched the extreme tantrums reduce over time to occasional blips in a happy, contented life. God ended my single mum journey in 2012 when I married a wonderful man who has been a Christian for over 30 years. God has answered prayer, and so often I am in awe of how faithful and generous He is. God chose to bring someone into my life who would teach me more of His ways and allow us to demonstrate to my children what a marriage with Christ at the centre looks like. In gaining a husband I also tripled the number of children in the home. There has been a lot more to learn and prayer has become a vital part of my day. Without a doubt, prayer is not just fundamental for the big decisions in life but essential for everyday living.

Seven months after marrying we decided it would be best I finished my part-time social work job and be full-time at home. With lots of gardens, a large home needing cosmetic work, a book to write and two families to settle, there would not be a shortage of things to do. Now, three and half years later I am on this last chapter and I have just received a call from my old workplace. So, I'm about to return to work with this book finished (well, at editing stage!), the garden looking a bit better and the home with new curtains and bathroom. The children are doing well despite the initial strain of blending and are enjoying school, university and work. God really does answer prayer.

My sister-in-law pointed out that God honours us when we make right choices. She saw that I had left work for the right reasons and that at the right time I was returning. I'll be honest, part-way through the job interview I wanted to run home and fold towels as it all seemed overwhelming. However, it is time for another season. The season at home has been amazing. Spending time in God's Word and doing Bible studies one-on-one and in small groups has been a unique and blessed time. It's highlighted to me the importance of establishing and building relationships with other women. It's not wise to isolate oneself too much but rather to find a healthy balance of home life and social life.

Hopefully my daughter's story in Chapter 8 has encouraged you to walk through any situation knowing that God is there for you and your children. What Jessie's story highlighted to me was the damage of divorce, and it challenged me to respond. The outcome has surprised me as I did not foresee that I would include a section on fighting for marriage, in this final chapter.

At the time when a marriage is barely surviving, it is easy to reject advice about sticking at it. In my situation, we did get some counselling and we had conversations about whether we wanted to give it another go. We decided at the time it wasn't right to stay together just for the sake of our children – that marriage needs to be a team. Another person had come into my husband's life and so we divorced.

I appreciate that while my marriage was not saved and yours may not be either, it saddens me whenever I hear someone wants to give up and not fight. I was so sad when a lady told me she wanted to leave her husband as she was not happy. Sadder still that she was inspired by how well she perceived I was doing as a single mother. Divorce is so hard on children – that's what I heard loud and clear on reading Jessie's story. I hope that when we hear of marriages in trouble, we urge and plead for them to get counsel and fight hard. While these interventions aren't guaranteed to work, my concern is that we can give up on the marriage too quickly. We can fall into the trap of thinking that life would be better without this person, or that it would be better to have a relationship with someone else. However, that someone else will still have their faults. That someone else will need to love and care for children who are not theirs. That's not always going to be easy. Whether the other person has children or not, they have their ways and views on parenting and life. There will be differences. There will be lots to work through and that person may not be as committed to your children as their biological parent, although this is not always the case.

When marriages dissolve with children involved, there is generally going to be an ongoing connection with their mum or dad. What is sad is when there is separation and for the rest of their lives the couple fight one another through family court, a lawyer, friends or their children. So let's be a voice advocating for marriage when our friends or family are struggling and ask us about our experiences. Let us be praying that families can work through their issues and come out stronger on the other side. I am encouraged by the guidance this quote gives us in such situations:

> Paul wrote to the Philippians that they should stop worrying and go to God with their requests. He follows by saying they were to dwell (reckon, measure, or deliberate) on things that are lovely, pure, and true. There is no one more true, lovely, excellent, and praiseworthy than God Himself. And there is no word more truer, purer, lovelier, or more excellent than the very words of God. There is nothing that can give us peace and joy like prayer, fixing our eyes on Jesus, and Scripture.[1]

I am very thankful for the wonderful years I had as a single parent of two great kids. Thankful for learning the importance and the blessing of being a parent. Just as God wrought much in me on that journey, He is doing the same in my new journey. Don't ever discount that God is doing a great work in you exactly where He has you right now. His Word states that He will 'equip you in every good thing to do His will' (Hebrews 13:21). Paul gives an example of His will: 'give thanks in all circumstances; for this is God's will for you in Christ Jesus' (1 Thessalonians 5:18, NIV). It is very much my prayer you will value your role very highly and wait on the Lord for His guidance. He knows us better than we know ourselves. Although it sounds like a cliché, I thought I would remain single for the rest of my days. I was okay with this; my life was full and content. As I reflect on this, I believe that dependence on Christ in our single parent role and leaning on Him for strength, makes a difference if He takes us through a blended family situation.

Sometimes, as we reflect on the past, we can appreciate the good times more clearly. While single parenting was sometimes difficult, with the benefit of hindsight I regret complaining. God knew His plans for me then and is still seeing them through. I had a great little fridge magnet to remind me: Grow wherever God plants you.

So ultimately our lives are in the hands of the author and finisher of our faith. I do hope you have been encouraged by reading this book and that together we can give all the thanks and glory to our great God. I would love to hear from you so please feel free to connect with me on my blog at Straight Paths Ministry (straightpaths.nz).

Appendix A

Becoming a Christian

Thank you for turning to the back of this book for an answer to this incredibly important question, 'How do I become a Christian?'

I knew so little when I gave my life to the Lord in 2006. I sat with my brother in McDonalds, Upper Hutt and as he talked he wrote on a piece of paper what becoming a Christian was all about. You can see his diagram on the next page.

The vertical line of dashes down the middle of the sketch represents a line of separation. On the left, marked A, is where all humanity is born, and according to Ephesians 2:1, we are born spiritually dead, we are alive physically but dead to God. Thus, the line of separation – our sin – has separated us from God according to Isaiah 59:2. The different denominations written under A and the arrow pointing to the church, shows that even if we are born into a 'religious' home, or are a church-going family, we are still dead and in need of being made alive (saved). All humanity is born on this side of the line, regardless of upbringing, church or no church, rich or poor, or nationality.

The group of words under B represent a time in one's life when we might be awakened to the possibility of God. Something happens in the family, we win lotto, a divorce happens or a can-

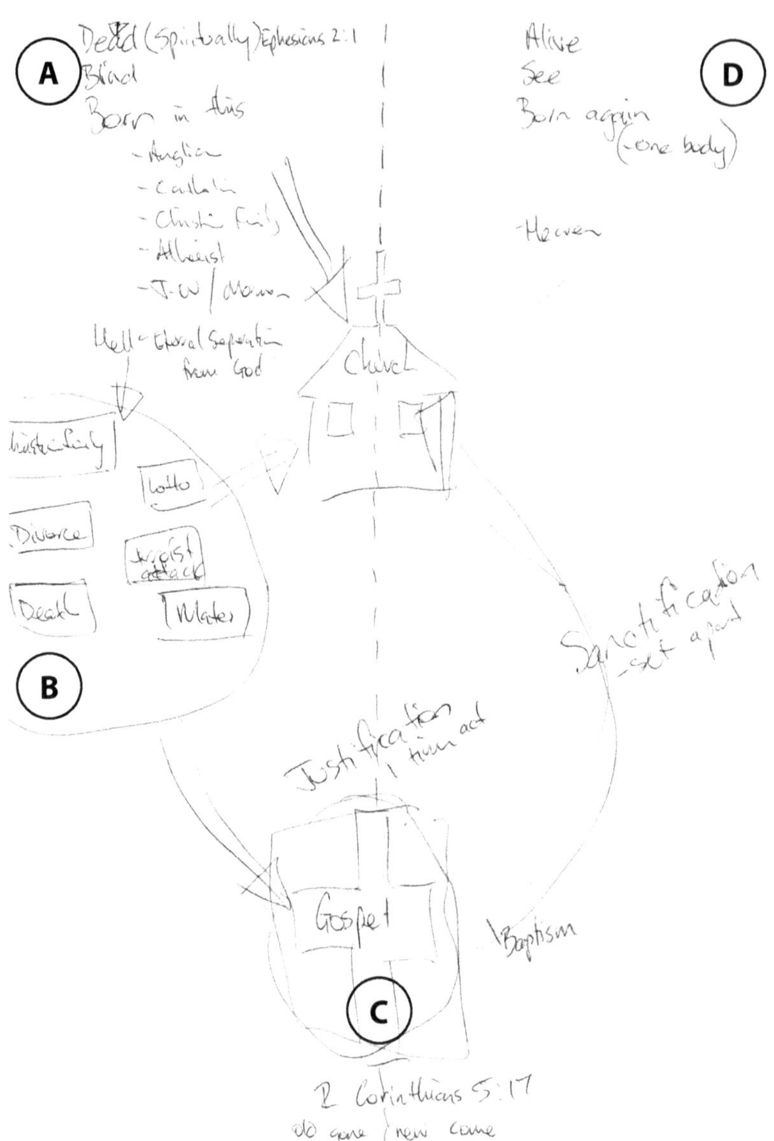
Dead (Spiritually) Ephesians 2:1
A
Blind
Born in this
- Atheist
Hell - Eternal Separation from God
Church
Lotto
Divorce
Death
B
Alive
See
Born again
(- one body)
D
- Heaven
Sanctification
- set apart
Justification
1 time act
Gospel
Baptism
C
2 Corinthians 5:17
old gone / new come

cer scare. And we ask the important question: what does God want or what is it that pleases Him? The arrow heading off to the church shows what many people decide God wants of us – to go to church. But notice the church crosses over the line of separation. Going to church at this point does not make you alive. The church does not save anybody. Humanity's problem is not that there is not enough religion; humanity's problem is that their sin has separated them from their maker and going to church does not deal with the sin problem. So what does?

The cross does, marked C. 'For God so loved the world that He gave His only begotten Son, that whoever believes in Him shall not perish but have eternal life' (John 3:16). Here is the good news for sinners (all of us). Humanity is born physically alive yet spiritually dead to God, their maker. The wages of our sin is death (Romans 6:23). No amount of good works, of giving money or of going to church and praying, can take away the sin and separation (see Ephesians 2:8-9). What sinners need is a Saviour. Jesus Christ is that Saviour, in fact He is the only Saviour (John 14:6; Acts 4:12). On the cross Jesus Christ bore our sin (1 Peter 2:24). His Father punished His Son as the sinner, and showed, through His death, burial and resurrection, that He was now satisfied that sin had been dealt with (Romans 4:23-25; 1 John 2:2 – propitiation means satisfaction). Sinners who repent of their sin and believe in Jesus Christ alone for their salvation will be saved. The only way to get across the line of separation is through the cross, where Jesus Christ died for sinners, that they might repent and believe.

Now that a sinner has come to the cross in repentance and belief, they are now on the right side of the line, marked D. They are known as new creations (2 Corinthians 5:17), they have been born again (made spiritually alive) (John 3:3). They have the presence of the Holy Spirit within them (Romans 8:9). They should be baptised (Matthew 28:19; Acts 2:38-41), and now church becomes real and meaningful.

I responded that I understood and accepted all that my brother had shared. I was excited. I had been given a small piece of paper with a prayer on it so I told him that I would pray for salvation and follow the Lord. A few days later when I knelt beside my bed, I prayed like this:

> Dear God, I know I'm a sinner, and I ask for your forgiveness. I believe Jesus Christ is Your Son. I believe that He died for my sin and that you raised Him to life. I want to trust Him as my Saviour and follow Him as Lord, from this day forward. Guide my life and help me to do your will. I pray this in the name of Jesus. Amen.[1]

Best day of my life ☺

Appendix B

A Dad's View

by Alan Lyford

When Jo initially asked me to write some material for her book I was in two minds. Firstly, I thought, *What can I offer?* I felt I had failed as a husband, I had ended up with a failed marriage – much like my own parents. Secondly, I battled with the idea that I would be seen as the enemy because, as a man, readers might associate me with their exes. Yes, I am a man – and the father of two beautiful children. I am a Christian who still fails and sins, – hopefully less than in the past. I have looked at the journey the Lord has taken me on over the last ten years by His grace and mercy. The Lord opened my eyes and showed me that it wasn't about me, it was about Him. So in response to Jo's request, here are some insights, not just from the other side of the fence as a divorced man, but also from the perspective of a father who wants to be actively involved in his children's lives. I hope you will be able to put aside the resentment you might feel towards any man who let you down, and allow me the opportunity to share some things that may help your children.

My story growing up

My family moved around New Zealand a lot when I was growing up. We even moved from the South Island, where most of our extended family lived, to the North Island. It wasn't until the end of my primary school years that my parents started attending a church in Stratford and taking us kids along. After a few years, on 21 October 1991, I became a Christian at a youth camp. I was baptised eight months later, just prior to moving to Upper Hutt.

Around this period and for the next six years, I experienced some tough times. My dad was away for weeks at a time travelling for work. Mum lost her driver's license after an accident, which made me the taxi driver for her and my siblings. I was 16 or 17 years old. I had become the 'man of the house' when Dad was away, and problems came a year or so later when he was home and returned to his role as father and husband. A couple of times it became physical between the two of us as I was now bigger than him.

With these pressures and challenges, I found it hard to settle into a new college and church. City life was different to the little country town I had been used to. Then the time came to study at a local tertiary institute. I had some new friends who weren't Christians and I was introduced to the drinking culture. The Lord protected me during this time as I was the designated driver when we went out.

I pondered what the future held for me and, as I started looking forward, my world just seemed to fall apart. My dad left my mum for another woman and moved out. I was back to resuming the role as man of the house. I started questioning my faith and the trust I had in people. I was struggling spiritually, emotionally and financially. I had just started a new job and was supporting Mum with mortgage payments as well as supporting my two younger siblings. As I tried to find out who I was in the midst of all this, I experienced some of my darkest hours. But by the grace of God, I can now see how He used these situations to grow and strengthen me for what was to come.

My own marriage story

I met my wife while helping out with the youth at a local Baptist church in Upper Hutt. We were involved in a youth outreach programme over the summer of 1999 and married in January 2000.

Financial pressure entered our marriage from the beginning as we continued to pay some of the mortgage on my family home as well as rent on our own house. Both of us had busy jobs and were making time for friends, family and youth work. At times life seemed great, other times really hard and sometimes somewhere in-between. Over a year later we discovered we were going to have our first child.

Throughout the pregnancy we were under the care of a specialist and everything seemed to be going well, as we understood it. It wasn't until the day our daughter was born that our world seemed to collapse from underneath us. Like any expecting parents, we believed everything was going to be fine. However, we discovered our daughter had Down syndrome and we were introduced to the world of the medical profession and a situation in which parents often have to fight for the well-being of their children. Life wasn't easy over the early period – some of our extended family were overseas and even sharing the news with our family was difficult.

Our little daughter wasn't well and we couldn't work out why. This put massive amounts of stress on my wife. She managed to breastfeed (not common for Down's kids), but the feeding was taking two hours and was physically draining. We ended up demanding that our paediatrician review our daughter's health and demanded that tests be done. The battle continued until finally it was discovered our daughter had a big hole in her heart. Within weeks we were in Greenlane Hospital and our daughter had heart bypass surgery. She was about nine months old. It was hard as a parent to see your child go through that; all I wanted to do was take her place. It was even harder for my wife as she heard comments such as, 'Didn't you know your daughter was going into heart failure as you breastfed her?'

A year later, our son was born. During that pregnancy a new battle with the medical profession began. They stated a one in 350 chance of our second child also having Down's. They told us we should have a test so we could terminate the pregnancy if required. We refused the test and trusted in the Lord as He knew what we could handle. Our son wasn't born with Down's.

Life was even busier than before. We were involved in a new church plant; I had started a new job which required some travelling and long days; and we were learning to live off one wage. My wife had done a great job being at home raising our kids, but I hadn't detected that her world had changed and she was struggling. To try to help and support her during this difficult period, I followed her to a new church where there were other families our age. As a result I stood down from being involved in the church plant we had helped to start. I found it hard not being involved every Sunday, but felt the move was necessary as I could see the joy my wife received from being amongst families with similar-aged children to ours.

Over the next couple of years I got more involved at the church and life was moving along; but it was so much harder than before the kids. My wife was still struggling and we knew our marriage wasn't perfect, but I thought we were doing okay. She suggested we get some counselling and, dragging my feet, I agreed. At first I didn't see the value, but I did learn to see it as a chance to share what we were really feeling. This wasn't easy for a guy with broken things from his past that he hadn't dealt with. I thought things were getting better after the counselling but sadly six months later my wife left.

Life after separation

Let's just say life wasn't easy. I had no clue what to do next. Come to a computer or business problem, I would be able to work it out and move on. But this ... I had no answers, plans, manuals or guides to help me out. I did have friends and the Word of God (the Bible).

It was about six months after my wife left that some friends suggested I go to a Christian conference called Impact. I registered at the last minute and went along having no clue what it was about. It was one of the hardest, most painful conferences I have ever attended, as I was forced to look at myself and deal with stuff. The conference theme that year was on marriage. The Lord broke me and started rebuilding me over that weekend with great teaching and friends by my side. I wished I had understood marriage, and my role in it, earlier in life. Maybe that could have held our marriage together.

More than ten years later, I can say life still has its ups and downs, but I enjoy being actively involved in my children's lives and watching them grow. I'm still single and my ex-wife has since remarried. We have a great co-parenting relationship with good, effective communication, talking almost every night for updates and discussions about the kids.

Life lessons

So what can I bring to the table after you have read this brief account of my life? These days I'm more aware it takes two to be in a relationship and two to work at it. I now know some of my shortcomings and how working on them, together with Christ, can help relationships to grow stronger. My first attempt at writing this was in isolation from Jo, but it was a blessing to see we had covered similar aspects of parenting – such as a need to communicate, examining ourselves and trusting in the Lord. So then the question became, what can I share from a father's point of view?

Father as spiritual leader: If the father of your children is a Christian and believes in the Word of God, he should be aware of his responsibility and be compelled to provide spiritual input to lead his children:

> This saying is trustworthy: 'If anyone aspires to be an overseer, he desires a noble work.' An overseer, therefore, must be above reproach, the husband of one wife, self-controlled, sensible, respectable, hospitable, an able teacher, not addicted to wine, not a bully but gentle, not quarrelsome, not greedy – one who manages his own household competently, having his children under control with all dignity. (If anyone does not know how to manage his own household, how will he take care of God's church?) (1 Timothy 3:1-5, HCSB)

This would mean the children attend church when they are with their father. As they get older and enjoy getting involved with church youth group activities, they may make their own decision to attend. Assuming the church is solid and teaches the Word of God well, your children's growing involvement should be encouraged.

Even if a father isn't a Christian, ideally he will be instructing his children to respect their mother – and mothers will teach their children to respect their father. This isn't always easy if you have been hurt and there is a level of fear and resentment. No matter what has happened between the parents, children need to know they are loved and learn to respect their parents. Here are some verses parents can teach their children about following instructions:

> Listen, my son, to your father's instruction, and don't reject your mother's teaching. (Proverbs 1:8, HCSB)

> Children, obey your parents as you would the Lord, because this is right. Honour your father and mother, which is the first commandment with a promise, so that it may go well with you and that you may have a long life in the land. Fathers, don't stir up anger in your children, but bring them up in the training and instruction of the Lord. (Ephesians 6:1-4, HCSB)

Son – the man of the house? I would like to expand on what Jo mentioned in Chapter 5 about being wise with the male company you keep. Sure, children need leaders – good role models in their lives they can look up to and learn from. But if you have a son, be aware that over time he might identify and take on the role of being 'the man of the house' when at his mum's place. He may see the need to protect everyone in the house, including his siblings and mother. This may cause some friction, which could escalate when another man comes on the scene. Depending on the age of your son, and the level of protectiveness he has for the family, this can become physical between them, or your son may choose not to be present when another man is in his mother's home.

If a new man is going to be in your life, I suggest you discuss the family structure with your son and what his role and responsibilities will be. He will want to protect you. Remember, this type of change may cause fear and hurt in children – especially if they are holding onto the hope that their mum and dad will get back together again.

Give each child individual time: I have learnt the importance of finding ways to spend one-on-one time with our children. This is important for developing trust and experiences for just the two of you. There are times when boys need to be boys, where a father and son can do things together. This is equally important for mothers and daughters; fathers and daughters; mothers and sons.

Individual attention becomes highly important if one of your children requires more time than the others. In my case, my Down syndrome daughter requires more time with tasks than my son. My daughter gets a lots of good, and bad, attention wherever we are and from whoever we are with. To ensure she doesn't have all of my time, taking me away from her brother, who can feel he's getting the leftovers, we organise times where his sister isn't with us. We do activities such as golf or football.

Make space to spend quality time together and allow it to be an opportunity to help understand what's really happening in your child's life. Without one-on-one attention your child may think they aren't important to you. Life is busy and things can get in the way, but we need to choose to put our family first. Spending time together gives opportunities to demonstrate love, respect, forgiveness, honesty and dependability. Try not to miss this opportunity otherwise they'll be all grown up and will have left home before you know it.

Changing the other person: You may think you can change your spouse, or former spouse, and may have even been trying to for some time. This doesn't work without first looking at yourself – especially when a relationship is under pressure. Consider examining yourself and the way you handle things. If we're not willing to make changes in our own lives, we cannot expect someone else to. If people see changes in our lives, this may have a positive effect on theirs.

The Word of God states in Romans 5 that we will face times of affliction. If we stand in our faith in Jesus Christ, we will grow and become the person Christ wants us to be.

> And not only that, but we also rejoice in our afflictions, because we know that affliction produces endurance, endurance produces proven character, and proven character produces hope. (Romans 5:3-4, HCSB)

Discipline: One issue that may arise as a result of separation is a mother's need to discipline her children when this was previously left to their father to enforce when he got home. Both parents need to be in agreement with the methods being used for discipline. Consider a few good, clear rules to be taught to your children. If these rules are broken, consistency in delivering the right level of correction is required. Have the correction fit the level of ill-discipline, without being unfair. The more consistent the discipline between the two homes, the better it will be for the children. This requires communicating a clear, consistent standard.

Having your time: Make sure you set aside time for yourself. It is important for you to study, reflect, talk to others and have time out, so that you can grow personally, grow stronger as a parent and recharge your battery. Raising children is draining, both physically and mentally.

While time with your children is precious and not to be neglected, you need to have energy and a mindset for teaching and equipping them. This is difficult to do effectively if you're not looking after yourself.

Routines: Children need constant and regular routines. This can be difficult when they are going between houses and particularly if you work extra hours to make ends meet. Children are more settled when there is a pattern in place for things like dinner time, bath or shower times, time for reading and talking and bedtime. Routine provides stability if worked at and agreed upon by both parents. This may not be an easy adjustment for the children's father. He may be used to working full-time, but not used to managing a household and the extra work required at the end of a working day.

This highlights the importance of having support and asking for help. Teaching children to manage the household and complete certain tasks is helpful as they get older, and this lightens our load as parents. It also equips them for their future home and in raising their own family. As well as addressing an it's-all-about-me, selfish mentality, children benefit from learning to see and help with other people's needs. This is a practical demonstration of love as described in 1 John:

> This is how we have come to know love: He laid down His life for us. We should also lay down our lives for our brothers. If anyone has this world's goods and sees his brother in need but closes his eyes to his need – how can God's love reside in him? Little children, we must not love with word or speech, but with truth and action. (1 John 3:16-18, HCSB)

Opportunity

As a final thought: going through separation and/or divorce is almost like having the same emotion and grief cycles as losing someone in death. One difference is that, when children are involved, you will see your ex again and again. This can bring up emotions over and over – different types of emotions at different times. The reason I mention this is that, on the positive side, this situation also gives you the opportunity to do something you cannot do if someone has passed away. You have a chance to talk to the other party about your regrets, and have the opportunity to forgive them and be forgiven. If you can come to that place, you will feel a weight lifted and a sense of freedom that may result in lessening the emotional roller coaster. If you are not yet able to reach that place, be encouraged to continue in prayer, seeking God's guidance and strength in this area.

It's not an easy thing bringing up children, but it can be one of the most rewarding tasks that you ever do in your life. Just remember you don't need to do it on your own when you are a part of God's family, 'For God has not given us a spirit of fearfulness, but one of power, love, and sound judgment.' (2 Timothy 1:7, HCSB)

Appendix C

Legislation

Two sections of New Zealand legislation are included in this appendix. Any mother not wanting to give access to her children's father needs to consider them. The legislation deals firstly with what is considered best for the child and, secondly, defines domestic violence.

Principles relating to child's welfare and best interests

The principles relating to a child's welfare and best interests are that –

(a) a child's safety must be protected and, in particular, a child must be protected from all forms of violence (as defined in section 3(2) to (5) of the Domestic Violence Act 1995) from all persons, including members of the child's family, family group, whānau, hapū, and iwi:

(b) a child's care, development, and upbringing should be primarily the responsibility of his or her parents and guardians:

(c) a child's care, development, and upbringing should be facilitated by ongoing consultation and co-operation between his or her parents, guardians, and any other person having a role in his or her care under a parenting or guardianship order:

(d) a child should have continuity in his or her care, development, and upbringing:

(e) a child should continue to have a relationship with both of his or her parents, and that a child's relationship with his or her family group, whānau, hapū, or iwi should be preserved and strengthened:

(f) a child's identity (including, without limitation, his or her culture, language, and religious denomination and practice) should be preserved and strengthened.

Section 5: replaced, on 31 March 2014, by section 4 of the Care of Children Amendment Act (No 2) 2013 (2013 No 74).[2]

Meaning of domestic violence[3]

(1) In this Act, ***domestic violence***, in relation to any person, means violence against that person by any other person with whom that person is, or has been, in a domestic relationship.

(2) In this section, ***violence*** means –
- (a) physical abuse:
- (b) sexual abuse:
- (c) psychological abuse, including, but not limited to, –
  - (i) intimidation:
  - (ii) harassment:

(iii) damage to property:
(iv) threats of physical abuse, sexual abuse, or psychological abuse:
(iva) financial or economic abuse (for example, denying or limiting access to financial resources, or preventing or restricting employment opportunities or access to education):
(v) in relation to a child, abuse of the kind set out in subsection (3).

(3) Without limiting subsection (2)(c), a person psychologically abuses a child if that person –
(a) causes or allows the child to see or hear the physical, sexual, or psychological abuse of a person with whom the child has a domestic relationship; or
(b) puts the child, or allows the child to be put, at real risk of seeing or hearing that abuse occurring; –
but the person who suffers that abuse is not regarded, for the purposes of this subsection, as having caused or allowed the child to see or hear the abuse, or, as the case may be, as having put the child, or allowed the child to be put, at risk of seeing or hearing the abuse.

(4) Without limiting subsection (2), –
(a) a single act may amount to abuse for the purposes of that subsection:
(b) a number of acts that form part of a pattern of behaviour may amount to abuse for that purpose, even though some or all of those acts, when viewed in isolation, may appear to be minor or trivial.

(5) Behaviour may be psychological abuse for the purposes of subsection (2)(c) which does not involve actual or threatened physical or sexual abuse.

Section 3(2)(c)(iva): inserted, on 25 September 2013, by section 5 of the Domestic Violence Amendment Act 2013 (2013 No 77).

Ideally shared access to children is amicably determined by both parents without involving the Family Court. When the Family Court is involved, affidavits may have to be written and these can be a hard, harsh document for others to read. Going through the Family Court can be a drain on all involved and, in my opinion, does not necessarily bring peace between parents.

The Government provides some practical resources on parenting through separation which include two, four-hour workshops. Parents do not attend together but will be given advice on how separation affects children; what's best for children when their parents no longer live together; and tools and tips for dealing with the situation, including how to make a parenting plan.[4] Workshops are run in most regions.

Birthright NZ is a well-respected non-government agency which can assist with a variety of issues including legal advice. Birthright 'believe[s] that all children have the right to a happy, secure and loving home environment ... and specialise[s] in working with families led by one person.' Their website (www.birthright.org.nz or phone 0800 457 146) is very informative and shows what is available in your region.

Notes

Introduction

1. Mackay, R. (2005). The Impact of Family Structure and Family change on Child Outcomes: A Personal Reading of the Research Literature. *Social Policy Journal of New Zealand Te Puna Wakaaro, 24*. Retrieved from www.msd.govt.nz/about-msd-and-our-work/publications-resources/journals-and-magazines/social-policy-journal/spj24/24-impact-of-family-structure-and-family-change-on-child-outcome-p111-133.html. Including Impacts on cognitive capacity (Fergusson, Lynskey and Horwood 1994), schooling (Evans et al. 2001), physical health (Dawson 1991), mental and emotional health (Chase-Lansdale et al. 1995), social conduct and behaviour (Morrison and Coiro 1999), peer relations (Demo and Acock 1988), criminal offending (Hanson 1999), cigarette smoking (Ermisch and Francesconi 2001), substance use (Fergusson, Horwood and Lynskey 1994), early departure from home (Mitchell et al. 1989), early-onset sexual behaviour (Ellis et al. 2003) and teenage pregnancy (Woodward et al. 2001).

Chapter 2: He Knows Me

1. Spurgeon, C. H. (1950). *The Treasury of David*, Vol. VI. Great Britain: Purnell and Sons. p. 258.

2. Gross W.H. (2005). Retrieved from http://livingsttonesclass.org/archive/davidchronolgygross.pdf
3. MacArthur, J. (2006). *The MacArthur Study Bible*, Nashville, TN: Word Bibles. p. 2022.
4. Spurgeon, *Treasury*. p. 259.
5. Ibid. p. 259.
6. Religious Tract Society's Commentary, quoted in ibid. p. 272.
7. Philpott, J.C., quoted in ibid. p. 272.
8. Ibid. p. 260.

Chapter 4: He Loves Me

1. *Repentance*: A change of mind which leads to a change of direction. The Hebrew word is *shuv* meaning to turn back to God, to change, and to restore. In Greek it is *metanoia* which means a change of mind. (e-Sword, Derivative Work, 2002-2014 by Rick Meyers.)
2. Spurgeon, *Treasury*. p. 262.
3. Bridges, J. (2007). *Respectable sins: Confronting the sins we tolerate*. Colorado Springs, CO: NavPress.
4. Weaver, J. (2006). *Having a Mary filled spirit: Allowing God to change us from the inside out*. Colorado Springs, CO: Waterbrook Press.
5. Biblical Counseling Foundation (2005). *Self-Confrontation Bible Study Student Workbook*. Palm Desert, CA: Biblical Counseling Foundation. p. W116.
6. Ibid. p. W180.

Chapter 5: He Protects Me

1. MacArthur, *Study Bible*, p. 1.
2. Adams, J. E. (1979). *A Theology of Christian Counseling: More than redemption*. Grand Rapids, Michigan: Zondervan.
3. MacArthur, *Study Bible*, p. 38.

4. Leupold, H. C. (1969). *Exposition of the Psalms.* Grand Rapids, MI: Baker Book House. p. 949.
5. Adams, J.E. (1972). *Christian living in the home.* Phillipsburg, NJ: Presbyterian and Reformed Publishing. p. 110.
6. Tripp, P. D. (2001). *Age of opportunity: A biblical guide to parenting teens.* Phillipsburg, NJ: Presbyterian and Reformed Publishing Company.
7. Biblical Counseling Foundation. *Self-Confrontation Bible Study Student Workbook.* p. W73.
8. Ibid. p. W174.
9. Lemmel, H. H. (1922).

Chapter 6: He Teaches Me

1. MacArthur, *Study Bible*, p. 862.
2. Ibid. p. 2009-2010.
3. Ibid. p. xxii-xxiii.
4. Biblical Counseling Foundation, *Self-Confrontation Bible Study Student Workbook.*
5. Ibid. p. W5.
6. Ibid. p. W160.
7. Thomas, A. (2007). *My Single Mom Life.* Nashville, TN: Thomas Nelson.
8. Ibid. p. xvi.
9. Tripp, T. (1995). *Shepherding A Child's Heart.* Wapwallopen, PA: Shepherd Press.
10. Sande, C. (1997). *The Young Peacemaker.* Wapwallopen, PA: Shepherd Press.
11. Ibid. p. 12.
12. McCaughrean, G. (2001). *John Bunyan's A Pilgrims Progress.* Victoria Embankment, London: Hachette Children's Group.
13. Meade, S. (2008). *Keeping Holiday.* Wheaton, IL: Crossway Books.

14. Wagnon, N. and Mills, B. (2012). *Checkpoints: A Tactical Guide to Manhood*. Colorado Springs, CO: NavPress.
15. Andreola, K. (1999). *Beautiful Girlhood*. Eugene, OR: Great Expectations Book Co.
16. Gresh, D. (2003). *Secret Keeper Girl: The Power of True Beauty and Modesty*. Chicago, IL: Moody Publishers.
17. Weaver, J. (2000). *Having a Mary Heart in a Martha World: Finding Intimacy with God in the Busyness of Life*. Colorado Springs, CO: Waterbrook Press.
18. Tripp, P. D. (2001). *Age of Opportunity: A Biblical Guide to Parenting Teens*. Phillipsburg. NJ: Presbyterian and Reformed Publishing Company.
19. DeMoss, N. L. and Gresh, D. (2009). *Lies Young Women Believe: And The Truth That Sets Them Free*. Chicago, IL: Moody Publishers.
20. Kassian, M. A. (2010). *Girls Gone Wise in a World Gone Wild*. Chicago, IL: Moody Press.
21. George, E. (2013). *A Girl's Guide to Making Really Good Choices*. Eugene, OR: Harvest House Publishers.
22. Bridges, J. (2007). *Respectable Sins: Confronting the Sins We Tolerate*. Colorado Springs, CO: NavPress Publishing Group.
23. MacArthur, J. (2004). *Experiencing the Passion of Christ: God's Purpose Behind Christ's Pain*. Nashville, TN: Thomas Nelson. p. 31.
24. Adams, J. E. (1989). *Christian Living in the Home*. Phillipsburg, NJ: Presbyterian and Reformed Publishing Company.
25. Adams, J. E. (1980). *Marriage, Divorce and Remarriage in the Bible*. Phillipsburg, NJ: Presbyterian and Reformed Publishing Company.
26. Grudem, W. (2009). *Bible Doctrine: Essential Teachings of the Christian Faith*. London, UK: SPCK Publishing.
27. Spurgeon, Vol. VI. p. 260.

Chapter 7: He Supports Me

1. Christians Against Poverty. See www.capnz.org
2. Peace, M. (1997). *Becoming a Titus 2 Woman*. Bemidji, MN: Focus Publishing. pp. 75,77.
3. Henry, M. (1714). *Commentary on the Whole Bible*. Retrieved from Meyers, R. e-Sword Version 11.0.6.
4. Retrieved from http://www.stats.govt.nz/Census/2013-census/profile-and-summary-reports
5. Weaver, J. (2000). *Having a Mary Heart in a Martha World*. Colorado Springs, CO: Waterbrook. p. 34.
6. George, E. (2003). *God's Wisdom for a Woman's Life*. Eugene, OR: Harvest House Publishers.
7. Peace, *Titus 2 Woman*. p. 49.

Chapter 9: He Answers Prayer

1. Biblical Counseling Foundation. *Self-Confrontation Bible Study Student Workbook*. p. W208.

Chapter 10: Final Reflections

1. Kendrick, S. & Kendrick, A. (2015). *War Room Bible Study*. Nashville, TN: Lifeway Press. p. 49.

Appendices

1. peacewithgod.net
2. Retrieved from legislation.govt.nz/act/public/2004/0090/latest/DLM317241.html
3. Retrieved from legislation.govt.nz/act/public/1995/0086/latest/DLM372117.html#DLM372117
4. www.justice.govt.nz/family/care-of-children/parenting-through-separation/

www.ingramcontent.com/pod-product-compliance
Ingram Content Group UK Ltd.
Pitfield, Milton Keynes, MK11 3LW, UK
UKHW020418250726
13967UKWH00007B/2712